C000009840

Comments on other *Amazing Stories* from readers & reviewers

"*Tightly written volumes filled with lots of wit and humour about famous and infamous Canadians.*"
Eric Shackleton, *The Globe and Mail*

"*The heightened sense of drama and intrigue, combined with a good dose of human interest is what sets* Amazing Stories *apart.*"
Pamela Klaffke, *Calgary Herald*

"*This is popular history as it should be... For this price, buy two and give one to a friend.*"
Terry Cook, a reader from Ottawa, on **Rebel Women**

"*Glasner creates the moment of the explosion itself in graphic detail...she builds detail upon gruesome detail to create a convincingly authentic picture.*"
Peggy McKinnon, *The Sunday Herald*, on **The Halifax Explosion**

"*It was wonderful...I found I could not put it down. I was sorry when it was completed.*"
Dorothy F. from Manitoba on **Marie-Anne Lagimodière**

"*Stories are rich in description, and bristle with a clever, stylish realness.*"
Mark Weber, *Central Alberta Advisor*, on **Ghost Town Stories II**

"*A compelling read. Bertin...has selected only the most intriguing tales, which she narrates with a wealth of detail.*"
Joyce Glasner, *New Brunswick Reader*, on **Strange Events**

"*The resulting book is one readers will want to share with all the women in their lives.*"
Lynn Martel, *Rocky Mountain Outlook*, on **Women Explorers**

GREAT MILITARY LEADERS

GREAT MILITARY LEADERS

Charismatic Canadian Commanders

MILITARY/HISTORY

by Norman Leach

To my wife Maritza and my daughter
Stephanie — without them this book would
never have seen the light of day.

PUBLISHED BY ALTITUDE PUBLISHING CANADA LTD.
1500 Railway Avenue, Canmore, Alberta T1W 1P6
www.altitudepublishing.com
1-800-957-6888

Copyright 2004 © Norman Leach
All rights reserved

Extreme care has been taken to ensure that all information presented in
this book is accurate and up to date. Neither the author nor the
publisher can be held responsible for any errors.

Publisher	Stephen Hutchings
Associate Publisher	Kara Turner
Series Editor	Jill Foran
Editor	Geoff McKenzie
Digital Photo Colouring	Bryan Pezzi

We acknowledge the financial support of the Government
of Canada through the Book Publishing Industry Development
Program (BPIDP) for our publishing activities.

Altitude GreenTree Program 🌲
Altitude Publishing will plant twice as many trees as were used
in the manufacturing of this product.

We acknowledge the support of the Canada Council for the Arts which
in 2003 invested $21.7 million in writing and publishing throughout Canada.

Canada Council   Conseil des Arts
for the Arts   du Canada

National Library of Canada Cataloguing in Publication Data

Leach, Norman, 1963-
   Great military leaders / Norman Leach.

(Amazing stories)
Includes bibliographical references.
ISBN 1-55153-773-7

1. Canada--Armed Forces--Officers--Biography. 2. Canada--
History, Military. I. Title. II. Series: Amazing stories (Canmore,
Alta.)

U54.C2L42 2004   355'.0092'271   C2004-902708-5

An application for the trademark for Amazing Stories™
has been made and the registered trademark is pending.

Printed and bound in Canada by Friesens
2 4 6 8 9 7 5 3

Contents

Prologue

The morning of June 2, 1916, dawned grey and drab. For the men of the Princess Patricia's Canadian Light Infantry, it felt like every other morning in Sanctuary Wood. Even the non-stop shelling from the German side was consistent. But by nine o'clock, it suddenly became very clear that this particular morning would be different after all. The shelling had increased to the point where it was a wall of steel falling on the Patricias and their founder, Major Hamilton Gault.

The German high-explosive shells churned the land, destroying everything in their path. Barbed wire, timbers, great clods of earth, and human bodies were thrown into the air as though caught in some unseen volcano. The Patricias knew this was only the first wave. After a shelling there was always an attack — always.

It was not long in coming. Before the smoke had even cleared, the Germans attacked. Soon the fighting was desperate hand-to-hand combat in the trenches, with victories determined at point-blank range or bayonet point. And as always, Major Gault was at the front.

Gault was looking over the battlefield, trying to find a way to stop the overwhelming German advance when a shell bowled him over, destroying his left leg and tearing apart his right. As he was carried from the battle, he passed out from the pain, only to wake a few minutes later to once again take command.

Lying on his stretcher, he calmly gave orders to his men, developing a defensive line among the chaos. When word came that the Germans had broken through, Gault remained on his stretcher with two revolvers in his hands, ready to meet the enemy.

But the enemy didn't make it to Gault and his stretcher; as the battle paused, stretcher cases were carried to the rear. Gault, pistols still in hand, refused to be evacuated until all of his wounded men were carried away. Then and only then did he allow the medics to pick up his stretcher.

As the stretcher-bearers carried Gault to a medical station, a splinter from a shell killed one of them. The major was thrown facedown into the mud, only to be picked up by two more men who finished the journey with Gault slung between them.

When he finally reached an aid station, it was clear to all present that Gault would lose his left leg. But to Gault, this seemed a small price to pay — his regiment had, once again, proven itself under fire.

Chapter 1

Lord Strathcona and Lord Strathcona's Horse

any of Canada's great military leaders were born into dynasties of wealth and privilege, but Donald Alexander Smith made his own way in the world. A descendant of the Grants of the Scottish Highlands, Smith would spend his life living the Grant family motto: "Stand fast."

Born in 1820, Donald Smith attended a private school in Forres, Scotland, and left with a well-rounded education. Upon graduation he apprenticed at a local lawyer's office, and in his later life reflected that, "the reason why poor Scots boys so frequently rose to distinction in all parts of the world is the native love for learning in even the humblest, and the excellence of the old-time Scottish schoolmasters."

Smith arrived in Canada in 1838 with little more than his education and his Scottish spirit. At that time, more than half of what is now Canada belonged to the Hudson's Bay Company (HBC), which owned and governed the vast territory to maximize profits — especially the profits of the fur trade. When the Dominion of Canada was created in 1867, Ontario was the dominion's westernmost boundary — everything to the west of that boundary, known as Rupert's Land and the North-West, belonged to the HBC.

Countless men who arrived in Canada throughout the 1800s found work with the HBC. Smith started his career as an apprentice clerk, counting muskrat skins at a salary of £20 a year, plus food. One of his primary duties was to ensure that the company accounts were up to date — a task he never quite mastered. He and the governor of the HBC, George Simpson, were at constant odds over the accounts, causing Smith great concern that he would be fired.

One night in 1846, while serving in the Mingan area of Quebec, Smith was working on the year's final accounts in his office. Meanwhile, in the adjacent barracks, a lit stove caused a chimney fire, which quickly spread throughout the building. Fearing that a year's worth of accounting would go up in smoke, Smith rushed into the fire and started to gather up all the papers he could. Heat and smoke singed his eyes as he tried to rescue the company's precious records. Driven back once by the heat, he charged again into the flames but was unable to retrieve more than a few scraps of paper.

Smith was forced to report to Governor Simpson that the records were lost and that he would need more time to present them, as he had to start all over again. Simpson was less than pleased, and the three-year-long feud over the accounts continued. For Smith, the ruined papers were only part of the disaster — his eyes were also badly burned in the fire. For a while, he had great difficulty seeing anything at all.

By 1847, Smith's eyes had not improved and in fact seemed to be getting worse. Of course, hunching over a factoring desk doing accounts by candlelight had not helped with the recovery process. Smith sent word to Simpson that he was going blind and that he needed to see a doctor in Montreal. Simpson, believing that Smith was simply trying to get out of completing that year's accounts, refused to grant him permission to make the journey.

But Smith, now convinced that he was indeed going blind, sent word to his boss that he would travel to Montreal with or without permission. Simpson declared that if Smith showed up in Montreal he would be relieved of his position in Mingan and would be reassigned to Labrador — an infamously difficult post within the company. Smith took the chance.

In Montreal, the doctor said that Smith's eyes were like "balls of fire," but concluded that no permanent damage had been done and that rest would solve the problem. Soon after seeing the doctor, Smith presented himself to Simpson, fully expecting to be fired. Instead, Simpson made good on his promise and ordered Smith to the Esquimaux Bay district of Labrador, insisting (according to legend) that he leave within

30 minutes — in the dead of winter.

To anyone in the service of the Hudson's Bay Company, being assigned to Labrador was considered banishment for life, and Smith briefly considered refusing his new assignment. However, he held his tongue, and started out for his new post, a journey that took months to complete and was made mostly on snowshoes.

While growing up in the Highlands of Scotland, Smith had learned the values of thrift and planning, and these values soon saw him promoted to chief trader at his new northern post. With his position secured, he married Isabella Sophia Hardisty, the daughter of a colleague working for the HBC. The couple established a new home in Labrador. Smith believed that Labrador could support the same type of farming economy as that of Northern Scotland. To prove his point, he imported cows, sheep, horses, and poultry, as well as garden and farm seeds. The lack of a long or warm growing season did not deter Smith. He fertilized his land with fish and successfully grew crops and flowers. Any plants that needed a longer growing season he cultivated in his greenhouse.

A practical man, Smith also established the habit of saving at least half of his income. As he rose through the ranks of the Hudson's Bay Company, he received a share of the profits and was able to save several thousand pounds, which he went on to invest in some of the largest and most profitable businesses in Canada. Soon, others were entrusting him with their savings, which he invested on their behalf. This allowed

Smith to gain a solid reputation and a growing influence in Canadian financial circles.

In 1862, Smith's life changed dramatically when he was transferred from Labrador to Montreal to assume the position of chief factor of the Hudson's Bay Company. Now one of the most powerful men in Canada, he was at the centre of Montreal's social and business elite at a time when the new Dominion was expanding at an unprecedented rate. It was a far cry from Labrador, where mail service was limited to two deliveries a year.

In Montreal he renewed his acquaintance with his cousin, George Stephen (later Lord Mount Stephen), who was a well-known and successful businessman in the city. Together the two cousins were soon investing in companies like the St. Paul, Minneapolis and Manitoba Railway and the Canadian Pacific Railway. Both men were destined to find fame and fortune.

But with Smith's growing fortunes came growing problems. Now in charge of the HBC's Montreal office, Smith was forced to deal with a crisis in the company and the country. The government of Canada, after purchasing the HBC's territory in the West in 1869, tried to extend its jurisdiction to the Red River settlement in present-day Manitoba. By that time, the area's population had grown to 12,000, and the Métis formed the majority of these settlers. Their leader, Louis Riel, defied the new governor who had been sent out to take over possession of the territory from the HBC. Riel then seized the HBC's Fort Garry, set up his own provisional government, and forwarded demands to Ottawa that the civil and land rights of the Métis be protected.

There was no way to move troops quickly to the West, and with the settlers' lives at risk, Ottawa had to do something. Smith, along with two other men, was selected by the federal government as a special commissioner and given the task of trying to pacify the rebellious settlers. Smith was a good choice, as he was respected by all concerned — including Riel.

When Smith arrived in what would become Manitoba, he immediately set out for Fort Garry — Riel's base of operations. As an official representative of the Canadian government, it would have been easy — and perhaps prudent — for him to have first sent someone ahead to ensure his personal safety. However, Smith was not one to let someone else take his risks, and, to the astonishment of the settlers, he grabbed the reins of a sleigh and headed the horses straight towards Riel's fort. He then walked up to the guards posted there and demanded, in French, to see Riel.

The surprised sentinels immediately sent for Riel, who appeared after a few minutes' delay. Smith was not impressed with the leader of the provisional government, and later described him as "a short, stout man with a large head, a shallow, puffy face, a sharp, restless, intelligent eye, a square cut, massive forehead overhung by a mass of long and thickly clustering hair and marked with well cut eyebrows —

altogether a remarkable looking face ..."

Riel, standing in the bitter cold, told Smith that he'd heard of his arrival in the territory and had just ordered his capture. Smith then calmly accompanied Riel to a room occupied by about a dozen men who were introduced as the provisional government. Riel demanded that Smith take an oath not to attempt to leave the fort that night or to upset their government. Smith, knowing that his task was to do exactly that, refused. He was placed in chains and sent to join the other English settlers Riel had arrested.

But Smith met with Riel daily, and slowly, through a force of will, convinced Riel that he would achieve more by working with the Canadian government than against it. Then, on a particularly frigid day, Smith addressed the population of the region. As icicles formed on his beard and his words clouded in ice vapour, he spoke to the settlers, asking them for calm. Recognizing that the English settlers in the area had some grievances with Ottawa as well, he worked hard to ensure that they did not join the Riel forces. Slowly, calm returned, and Riel — believing that Smith was really on his side — allowed the English settlers he'd imprisoned to be released from custody.

The English settlers immediately started feuding with Riel's provisional government and, after a series of scuffles, a Métis hunter ended up killing a young Englishman, further inflaming the settlers against Riel. Gathering up arms and horses, the English settlers marched on Fort Garry. Although calmer heads began to prevail, a small group of angry settlers under Captain Charles Boulton insisted on attacking Riel, despite Boulton's arguments to the contrary.

As the settlers neared the fort, Boulton ordered that no shots be fired, and the Métis appeared just as accommodating, inviting the group inside to discuss their grievances. However, immediately upon entering the fort, the settlers were captured and disarmed. A tribunal quickly ordered that Boulton be put to death.

When Smith heard of the sentence he went to Fort Garry and demanded to see Riel. In Smith's words, "Riel was obdurate and said that the English settlers and Canadians had laughed at and despised the French Half Breeds, believing that they would not dare to take the life of anyone, and that, under the circumstances, it would be impossible to have peace and establish order in the country; an example must therefore be made, and he had firmly resolved that Boulton's execution should be carried out, bitterly as he deplored the necessity of doing so."

Smith argued with Riel that the death of Boulton would only enrage Canada, and that the government would be forced to act militarily against Riel and his followers. Riel finally agreed to release the prisoners on the condition that Smith help pacify the English settlers and work with him to solidify his government.

Thinking that things were finally under control, Smith began to pack his bags for his return to Ottawa. However, only four days later he was brought the news that instead of releasing all of the prisoners, Riel was now contemplating executing a second man, Thomas Scott. An unruly prisoner, Scott had baited Riel with racial insults and slights questioning his courage. Despite warnings from Riel, Scott had persisted with his taunts, until finally, on March 1, 1870, Riel sentenced him to death.

Smith raced to Fort Garry to try to dissuade Riel from allowing the execution to take place, but it was of no use. Riel believed that he needed to set an example that would "oblige other impetuous and bigoted young men to curb their tongues and tempers."

Observers later reported that a firing squad of six Métis, commanded by Riel, shot and killed Scott. This convinced Smith that there was no longer any reason for him to stay in the region — the government of Canada would never negotiate with Riel now that he had allowed a man to be deliberately killed.

That summer, the forces sent by the Canadian government arrived in the region to be greeted by Smith, who had returned to the area to take a hand in governing the region once Riel was defeated. But the Canadian force, led by Garnet Wolesely, never fired a shot. Recognizing that he was facing a vastly superior force, Riel abandoned his provisional government and fled to the United Sates.

With the rebellion safely dismantled, Smith next set his sights on public office. He was elected to the Legislative

Assembly of Manitoba, representing Winnipeg and St. John, and served from 1871 until January 1874. In those days, it was also possible in Canada for one man to hold both a provincial and federal seat, so Smith ran federally and was elected to the Dominion Parliament representing Selkirk, Manitoba, in 1871. Though he was re-elected several times throughout the 1870s, he was defeated in 1880. Nevertheless, in 1887, he returned to Parliament representing western Montreal — an office he would hold until retiring in 1896.

In addition to his political success, the 1870s saw Smith flourish as a businessman and a nation builder. After Confederation, many Canadians believed that the United States would annex both the western prairies and British Columbia — perhaps even the whole of the Dominion. Prime Minister Sir John A. Macdonald wrote that he was "convinced beyond any doubt that the United States Government was resolved to do all it could, short of going to war, to obtain possession of Western Canada."

With only a few thousand citizens in the West, neither Canada nor England could have mounted a real defence, as the only way for troops to reach the territory in winter was through the United States.

Like Prime Minister Macdonald, Smith recognized that a military solution was out of the question. Both men instinctively embraced a more constructive solution: a transcontinental railway linking the west with the east. It was an opportunity to build the nation and, for Smith in particular, to profit.

When Smith and his cousin Stephen bought the half-built but abandoned St. Paul and Pacific Railroad, they may have had visions of "an unbroken series of colonies, a grand confederation of loyal and flourishing provinces" stretching from the Atlantic Ocean to the Pacific Ocean, but they were mostly interested in profit. When the St. Paul and Pacific was completed in 1878, Smith was gratified to see the predicted invasion of Americans. Settlers and farmers anxious to buy up the cheap land in the new province of Manitoba flooded the region. For Smith and Stephen, the profits poured in.

British Columbia, promised a rail connection to the rest of Canada within 10 years, joined Confederation in 1871. But the promise would be a long time in coming, as the decade was marked by political turbulence. Prime Minister MacDonald's government was defeated, and Alexander Mackenzie's Liberals did not feel a need to keep Conservative promises. When Macdonald was re-elected in 1882, the government chose the syndicate headed by Smith and Stephen to build what would become known as the Canadian Pacific Railway (CPR). That same year, the CPR hired William Cornelius Van Horne to build a rail line that many believed could not be built.

In November of 1885, after years of arduous work, the railway was completed. On November 7, railway workers and officials from across the nation gathered at Craigellachie in B.C.'s Eagle Pass to watch as Smith drove in "the last spike." On June 28, 1886, the first train scheduled to make the cross-

Canada run pulled out of the station in Montreal. The CPR had accomplished the "Canadian Dream," linking the settled eastern cities with the Pacific. There was no more talk of British Columbia leaving the Dominion.

In 1886, Queen Victoria announced that Smith would receive a knighthood of the Order of St. Michael and St. George in recognition of his work on the railroad. Sir Donald did not see the knighthood as the pinnacle of his career, but as just one more step on what had already been a long road. The knighthood seemed to spur him on to even greater acts of philanthropy at a time when he was seen as one of the most generous men in Montreal.

For a man who once scrimped to save half of his meagre salary each year, Sir Donald had become a wealthy and generous philanthropist. Throughout his life he made many contributions both publicly and anonymously. In 1887, together with his cousin Lord Mount Stephen, he set aside one million dollars to erect a free hospital in commemoration of Queen Victoria's Jubilee. Over his lifetime, Smith would give many millions of dollars to charities across Canada and around the world. To the very end he had a great sympathy for human suffering, and medical charities were always near and dear to his heart.

In 1896, at the age of 76, Sir Donald Smith was named the third High Commissioner for Canada to London — a position he held for 18 years. As the high commissioner, it was Sir Donald's responsibility to ensure that Canada's interests were represented at court and in Parliament.

Even before he left Canada, it was announced that Smith was to be promoted from Knight Commander to Knight Grand Cross of the Order of St. Michael and St. George, and that the award would be presented by Queen Victoria herself. This required Sir Donald to become a very public person in London, as the award carried with it the possible promotion to the peerage — there was a chance for him to become a Lord.

Sir Donald's strong personality impressed everyone who saw and heard him. He spoke anywhere and everywhere on the land, culture, business, and opportunities in Canada. Serving on a number of special commissions that examined the relationship between England and its colonies, he was always a strong proponent of imperial unity. Sir Donald's overarching goal as high commissioner was to strengthen the ties between Canada and Britain.

London society was taken with this Canadian, and he was soon one of the best-known and most popular figures in the public life. By the spring of 1897, after Whitehall and Windsor Castle had had an opportunity to see the impact Sir Donald was having in London and across England, it was finally decided to raise him to the peerage. There was another reason for the decision: Queen Victoria was celebrating her Diamond Jubilee and wanted to use the celebrations to recognize and honour persons of distinction across her empire.

Smith was required to choose a name for his peerage,

and many thought he would become Lord Glencoe, after his vast sporting estate in Scotland. As usual, he did not do the expected and chose the title of Lord Strathcona and Mount Royal of Glencoe, in the County of Argyll, and of Mount Royal in the Province of Quebec and Dominion of Canada.

* * *

The Boer War, at the end of Queen Victoria's reign, gave the new Lord Strathcona an opportunity to once again provide service to Canada and the British Empire. In January 1900, he offered to pay for a mounted regiment to serve in South Africa. His letter to Prime Minister Laurier read: "Should like to provide and send to South Africa my personal fund squadron mounted men and officers say 400 men and horses from North West, single men if possible. Force will be Canadian but distinct from Government contingent. Men must be expert marksmen, at home in saddle, efficient as rough riders and rangers. I propose pay cost shipment similar to that of Canadian Contingent and transport if you approve proposal. Would like use of Government organization for recruiting force, if that is practicable."

Lord Strathcona's only request was that his donation be accepted as an anonymous one. He wanted the donation of the mounted regiment to be seen as a gift from Canada and not from himself.

On January 3, 1900, the government of Canada agreed

Lord Strathcona's Horse, under inspection in Ottawa, March 1900.

to Lord Strathcona's proposal. He immediately authorized the commander-in-chief of the army in Canada to use up to £150,000 to equip a mounted force that would be contributed to the Imperial Forces. Lord Strathcona would be responsible for the regiment until it arrived in South Africa. After that, it would be under the control of the British Army.

There was no way to keep such a generous offer secret from the media or the public. Lord Strathcona was embarrassed, and angry, when he was revealed in newspapers as the "mysterious donor." His desire for secrecy came from long experience in government, business, and diplomatic circles, and he once remarked to a friend that, "nothing is secret when more than one knows it."

With this particular secret now very public, it was decided to name the regiment "Lord Strathcona's Horse." The toughest men in Western Canada were recruited. Cowboys, North-West Mounted Police officers, and anyone who could ride a horse rushed to join. All of the officers and men enlisted for a six-month tour of duty with the possibility of an extension to a full year.

Once enough soldiers were recruited, the regiment travelled to Ottawa for training at Lansdowne Park. As they paraded on Parliament Hill, the men painted quite a picture with their stetsons, ponies, western saddles, and lassos. By any measure, they were not Queen Victoria's typical soldiers.

Lord Strathcona's Horse arrived in Cape Town on April 10, 1900, with a complement of 28 officers, 518 non-commissioned officers and men, and 599 horses. Though the soldiers were anxious to join the battle before "the war ended and we had not seen any action," an outbreak of disease among the horses confined the regiment to camp.

In June, the regiment found itself part of General Buller's Natal Field Force (3rd Mounted Brigade), which was in the Transvaal trying to run the Boers to ground. Tasked as scouts, the regiment often rode far in advance of the troops and were the first to make contact with the enemy, suffering extensive casualties as a result.

On the week of July 1, Dominion Day in Canada, the Strathconas engaged in three skirmishes that would result in 15 Canadian casualties and claim several Boer lives. It was a fair introduction of things to come — the Strathconas spent most of their six-month tour engaged in skirmishes and battles with irregular Boer mounted riflemen and guerrillas.

The regiment acquired a reputation for bravery, as evidenced by a citation for one Sergeant Arthur Richardson: "On 5 July 1900 at Wolwespruit, Standerton, South Africa, a party of Lord Strathcona's Horse (38 in number) came into contact and was engaged at close quarters with a force of 80 of the enemy. When the order was given to retire Sergeant Richardson rode back under very heavy cross-fire, picked up a trooper whose horse had been shot and who was badly wounded and rode with him out of fire. This act of gallantry was performed within 300 yards of the enemy and Sergeant Richardson was himself riding a wounded horse." Sergeant Richardson was awarded the Victoria Cross for his valour.

By January of 1901, the Strathconas were on their way home, having done their duty. But first, Lord Strathcona had a special surprise for his boys. He had convinced King Edward VII to present the King's colours to the mounted force. The men were doubly surprised, as the ceremony was usually restricted to infantry units.

King Edward also took the opportunity to present the Strathconas with their South African Campaign medals.

Lord Strathcona and his horse, Trooper, ca. 1900

The men thanked their obviously proud benefactor — many were meeting him for the very first time.

Upon their return home, the regiment was recognized as having done exemplary duty in the Boer War. Unfortunately, this did not prevent the government from disbanding Lord Strathcona's Horse. Then, as now, Canadian defence policy was often driven by financial rather than military considerations. Cavalry regiments were expensive to maintain, and the government believed that with no evident threat, it would be too expensive to retain the Strathconas.

However, in 1909, with tensions increasing in Europe,

the regiment was re-formed and named Lord Strathcona's Horse (Royal Canadians) — LdSH(RC). When World War I began, the Strathconas were once again called to duty. After training in England, the regiment was sent to France to serve as much needed infantry. For a cavalry unit, it was a difficult task to accept, and the Strathconas were happy to become a mounted force again in 1916.

On March 27, 1917, the Strathconas would win another Victoria Cross. This time it would be Lieutenant Frederick Harvey who would do his regiment proud. The official citation read: "During an attack by his regiment on a village (Guyencourt in France) a party of the enemy ran forward to a wired trench just in front of the village and opened rapid fire and machine gun fire at very close range, causing heavy casualties in the leading troop. At this critical moment when the enemy showed no intention whatever of retiring, and while fire was still intense, Lieutenant Frederick Harvey, who was in command of the leading troop, ran forward well ahead of his men, and dashed at the trench (still fully manned), jumped the wire, shot the machine gunner, and captured the gun."

And this was not the Strathconas' only Victoria Cross of the conflict, either. About one year later, Lieutenant Gordon Flowerdew would lead one of the last true cavalry charges of the war. His official citation described the battle on March 31, 1918 at Moreuil Wood:

"Lieutenant Gordon Flowerdew saw two enemy lines, each about 60 strong, with machine guns in

the centre and flanks. One line was about 180 metres behind the other. Realizing the critical nature of the operation and how much depended on it, Flowerdew ordered a troop under Lieutenant Harvey to dismount and carry out a special movement while he led the remaining three troops to the charge.

"The squadron passed over both enemy lines, killing many of the enemy with the swords and wheeling about galloped at them again. Although the squadron had then lost about 70 percent of its numbers, killed and wounded, from rifle and machine-gun fire directed on it from the front and both flanks, the enemy broke and retreated. The survivors of the squadron then established themselves in a position where they were joined, after much hand-to-hand fighting, by Lieutenant Harvey's party. Lieutenant Flowerdew was dangerously wounded in both thighs during the operation but continued to cheer his men on."

The next day, Flowerdew died in hospital as a result of his wounds. He was awarded the Victoria Cross posthumously.

* * *

Sadly, Lord Strathcona himself was not alive to share the glory with the regiment that bore his name — though he didn't miss it by much.

Lord Strathcona remained a vigorous overachiever well into his 90s. At an age when most men would have sat back and enjoyed their wealth and prestige, he purchased a great sporting estate at Glencoe. When he wasn't there he was back in London, where he would often be found working, the lights burning brightly in his office on Victoria Street, late into the night. Lady Strathcona, always the protector, would frequently arrive at his office with a picnic basket, reminding him to eat dinner.

In the early autumn of 1913, Lord Strathcona paid what would be his last visit to his Glencoe estate and then returned to London with Lady Strathcona. That November, Lady Strathcona contracted what doctors diagnosed as a common cold. However, the "cold" developed into influenza and pneumonia, and five days later, she died. Lady and Lord Strathcona had been married for more than 60 years.

Lord Strathcona did not survive his wife long. The "Grand Old Man of Canada" died on the January 21, 1914. He was buried next to Lady Strathcona in Highgate Cemetery, London.

Chapter 2

Lieutenant Colonel George Taylor Denison III and the Governor General's Body Guard

hen Gilbert and Sullivan wrote the famous musical *The Pirates of Penzance*, they created a gentleman officer who was the "very model of a modern Major-General." While it is doubtful the British duo ever met Lieutenant Colonel George Taylor Denison III, they could certainly have been writing about the man who led the Governor General's Body Guard (GGBG) in Canada for most of Queen Victoria's reign.

Denison was the perfect Victorian military officer, coming from a prominent military family and even claiming ties, through marriage, to the United Empire Loyalists. The colonel was just over 5 feet, 11 inches tall and weighed 148 pounds, cutting a fine figure in his cavalry uniform. He sported the requisite moustache and had the piercing gaze of a man meant to command.

Born at his family's home in Toronto, Ontario, on August 31, 1839, it was clear from the beginning that George Taylor Denison III was going to be a cavalry officer. His great grandfather, Richard Lippincott, had fought with the Loyalists during the American Revolution. His paternal grandfather, Lieutenant Colonel George Taylor Denison I, had been a sergeant in the War of 1812 and later formed the York Dragoons, a cavalry corps in Toronto. His father, George Taylor Denison II, was also a member of the York Dragoons, and had helped put down a rebel force in London, Ontario.

But of all the military men in his family, George III's maternal grandfather, Jeremiah Dewson (a veteran of Waterloo), was perhaps the most influential. While he was growing up, George would often spend his after-school hours in the company of Grandfather Dewson learning to ride, shoot, and use the cavalry sabre.

The lessons paid off — in 1854, at the age of 15, George was appointed coronet of the Denison Cavalry Troop, and in 1856 he was gazetted (named) a lieutenant. By 1857, he was in temporary command of the troop and later that year became a captain. He was given permanent command of the troop when he was just 17 years old. (The Denisons themselves made the appointments, but they nevertheless had to be approved by military authorities.)

In 1855, the new Militia Act came into force, which gradually gave the government of Canada the responsibility of its own defence. For an ambitious Canadian cavalry officer, the British withdrawal was a heaven-sent opportunity, and the young Denison leapt at the chance to better his position in life. When the government told him he would not be able to keep his rank under the new system unless he could bring the cavalry troop up to full strength, he recruited a full complement of troops (about 60) and started to outfit them.

But Denison hit a snag early in the process. While the government agreed to provide new swords, belts, pouches, and Colt revolvers for each man, it would not provide saddles and bridles. To any cavalry officer, it was essential that a troop matched in every detail. Because the officers were already paying for the uniforms, Denison thought the least the government could do was provide the saddles and bridles. The government refused, insisting it was tradition for Canadian militia officers to outfit their men, and this included providing them with saddles. Denison could not dispute this claim — he recalled complaints from both his father and grandfathers recounting the same stingy treatment at the hands of the government.

As the Canadian government remained steadfast in its refusal to provide him with saddles and bridles, Denison took it as a personal slight against his family and himself. So began a long-simmering feud between Denison and the government that the young man would never get over.

Denison came by his obstinacy honestly, at least according to the experts of the time. In 1859, phrenology was all the rage. Practitioners of the new "science" believed that by feeling and "reading" the bumps on a person's head it was possible to not only understand a person's personality but also his or her future. Denison travelled to New York City to consult with Professor L.N. Fowler, the world's leading phrenologist. After reading the bumps on Denison's head, Fowler told him that he was "industrious, ambitious, decidedly wilful [sic] and of a romantic class of mind, though lacking somewhat in dignity and too stubborn." Fowler assured Denison that he would "yet take hold of some public enterprise and gain reputation where it requires some uncommon vigour and resolution."

But Denison's reputation at Toronto's prestigious Upper Canada College, where he studied, was less flattering. He proved to be an indifferent student — his only real passion was military history.

After graduating, he enrolled in law at Trinity College in Toronto. In keeping with Professor Fowler's assessment of his stubborn nature, Denison was thrown out of the college for "being rude to one of his masters." Despite his father's best efforts, he was not reinstated. He finished his education at the University of Toronto and was called to the Ontario Bar in 1861. He then began his law practice.

To Denison, the law was simply a way to make a living. He was, and always would be, a cavalry officer — and an author. In 1861, his first of a long line of published works, "The National Defences," was well received by the general public. In 1862, he was named brevet major for the Denison Cavalry Troop and was well on his way to becoming a full-time, professional cavalry officer and military historian.

On January 20, 1863, Denison married Caroline Macklem, the granddaughter of one of the richest men in the Niagara Peninsula. The happy couple felt comfortable enough financially to build a home, "Heydon Villa," on the Denison estate in Toronto. Denison was ready to embrace his role as a lawyer, a cavalry officer, and the descendant of one of Upper Canada's most respected families.

Success, however, did not come easily — mostly because of Denison's own legendary stubbornness. Once he picked a cause, however unpopular, he stuck by it, regardless of the political consequences to himself.

One such cause was the American Civil War. Like most Canadians, he supported the Confederacy — he worried that a Northern victory would mean the end of British North America. Further, Denison was personally taken with the Confederates, seeing in them the best of the cavalier traditions he held so dear. Besides, Denison's uncle, George Dewson, was a colonel in the Confederate Army, and to Denison, blood ran thick.

Colonel Dewson came to Toronto in September of 1864 and stayed at Heydon Villa with Denison and Caroline. Dewson's orders were to "evaluate potential British North American support for the Confederacy." Suddenly, Denison's family connections, as well as his position and role as an active officer in the cavalry, made him an important player in the Confederate movement. Soon, every Confederate sympathizer who sojourned in Toronto turned up at Heydon Villa. The Denison home became known openly as the final stop for Confederate spies as they carried information throughout the North.

Colonel Jacob Thompson, the senior Confederate officer in Toronto, was a regular visitor, and he and Denison became close friends — so close that Denison was apparently admitted to the "Band of Brothers" who carried out raids on Vermont and firebomb attacks on New York in 1864. (History does not reveal what role Denison played in the attacks, or whether he was even present.)

Colonel Thompson had a problem, and he fingered Denison as the solution. In November 1864, Thompson had arranged for the Confederacy to purchase a steamship named the *Georgian*. His intention was to refit the ship as a Great Lakes raider to attack federal targets of opportunity along the lakeshores. But when the *Georgian* sailed from Port Colbourne, she was intercepted by an American coast guard vessel. Federal sympathizers had warned the coast guard that the *Georgian* was on her way to bombard Buffalo, New York.

When the *Georgian* was boarded by American Federal authorities, her crew was drunk and there were no guns onboard — so naturally, she was allowed to continue on her way. Arriving in Collingwood, Ontario, on December 7, the ship was detained by Canadian Customs officials. The

Canadians were on the lookout for suspicious activity after a cannon had mysteriously disappeared from the Guelph, Ontario, town square. Further, a Confederate sympathizer in Guelph had been discovered making shot and munitions to fit the missing cannon.

When the shot, cannon, and *Georgian* all arrived on the same day in Collingwood, even the Canadians, who were reluctant to get involved, had to act. The only hope the Confederacy had of saving the ship was to sell her to a British subject — and the best friend of the Confederacy in Canada was Major G.T. Denison.

In January 1865, the *Georgian* was released to Denison. However, in April of the same year, the U.S. government argued that Denison did not really own the ship, but was only holding it for the Confederacy. To bolster this argument, the American consul general, David Thurston, presented intelligence to the Canadian government that Denison and William MacDonald, the transportation agent for the Confederacy in Toronto, were altering the *Georgian* so that it could carry a cannon.

When officials boarded the *Georgian* in Collingwood they found Denison and MacDonald hard at work at what was later described as "suspicious activity." Even more suspicious were the torpedoes and other munitions that turned up under Thompson's floorboards when his house was raided. The *Georgian* was again seized by Canadian officials.

Angry, Denison launched a case at the Court of Queen's

Bench to reassert his ownership claim. But in 1866, the courts ruled that he was to turn the *Georgian* over to the U.S. government.

Denison, who saw an opportunity to profit from the sale of the *Georgian* slip through his fingers, immediately demanded that he be compensated for the loss of the vessel. His price was to be named a Conservative candidate for the new Parliament in the riding of West Toronto. Prime Minister Sir John A. MacDonald suggested, instead, that Denison accept the post of adjunct general for cavalry in the new Dominion of Canada.

But before the prime minister and Denison could come to an agreement, all of the Dominion's militia forces were called out to protect Canada during the Fenian Raids of 1866. Denison's political ambitions would have to wait.

* * *

The American Irish Republican Army, a group of mostly ex-Federal Irish soldiers in the U.S., came up with a plan to invade Canada. They believed that if they, the "Fenians," attacked Canada, Britain would be forced to send extra troops to defend the Canada–U.S. frontier. This, in turn, would cause a shortage of troops in Ireland and allow for a general revolution there. The plan was doomed from the very start.

In June 1866, the Fenians crossed the Niagara River at

Fort Erie, and the whole militia force of Upper and Lower Canada was ordered out. Denison knew that his opportunity as a cavalry officer had arrived. This fight was personal. Still disgruntled at his treatment by the American government during the *Georgian* affair, he saw a chance to strike a blow for Canada and to personally win a victory over the Fenians — most of whom were Northerners who had fought against the Confederacy.

Denison immediately sent word to the commanding officer, Major General Napier, that his troop, officially renamed in April the Governor General's Body Guard of Upper Canada, was ready to go immediately. But as morning stretched to afternoon without word from the major general, Denison grew frustrated. He knew Napier's forces would need "eyes and ears," and cavalry were ideally suited to act as scouts. The longer Denison was allowed to stew, the angrier he got. He was convinced that the government was again punishing him for his role in the *Georgian* affair.

There is no record as to why Napier waited so long to respond to Denison, but he was preparing for an imminent invasion of Canada, after all. At 3:00 p.m. on Friday, June 1, the Body Guard was finally ordered to the front — the last corps ordered out of Toronto. By midnight, the Body Guard was gathered together and ready to move out, even though some of the men lived more than 20 kilometres apart.

Despite their readiness, the men of the Body Guard were ordered to wait until 7:00 the next morning for a steamer, the *City of Toronto*, to transport them across Lake Ontario to the Niagara frontier. On their arrival, the Body Guard was ordered to proceed immediately to Port Robinson via the Welland Railway. Denison and his men realized that cavalry would be needed as quickly as possible to assist at the front. Wasting no time, Denison took charge of assembling a train to carry his force to Port Robinson, the closest point to Chippewa, where he knew the battle would take place.

Upon arriving at Port Robinson, the Body Guard unloaded the train and immediately marched for Chippewa. However, this was cavalry, and both the men and horses needed to be watered and fed when they arrived. Within two hours, all 30 horses were fed, watered, and even re-shoed.

After a march to the town of New Germany, the Body Guard was sent forward to form an advance guard. But still, the Body Guard's progress was delayed by what Denison saw as pointless protocol. They were ordered to keep pace with the infantry who were also marching to the front, though it was clear to Denison that the cavalry should scout ahead.

At dusk, Denison and the Body Guard finally came into contact with the Fenians and called a halt. Scouts were sent out on both sides of the road, and they reported that the Fenians had added reinforcements. However, the Americans did not fire. Denison was convinced that the main Fenian force was on alert and that the woods needed to be searched to prevent an ambush. But, as he later noted, it had grown so dark "that the men could not, in the woods, see from one to the other; and there being a great deal of tangled bush and logs, and being very marshy and wet, the men could make no headway whatever."

That night, the men of the Body Guard lay on both sides of the road and in the field nearby — fully dressed with their horses saddled. In the morning, Denison was proven right — the main Fenian force had been on alert and ready to ambush the Canadians. But when Denison and the Body Guard moved forward at first light, the enemy posts were abandoned. The enemy had retreated in the night to Fort Erie, where they reported that British cavalry had attacked them.

Through the ages, cavalry had always frightened infantry, and it took a well-trained infantry unit to stand against the horses and flashing swords of a cavalry charge. The Fenians were far from well trained, and as word of cavalry spread, so did panic among them. Most made the swift decision to retreat across the river back to Buffalo. According to a reporter for the *Buffalo Express*, who was with the Fenians: "The retreat was so rapid that rowboats were then crossing the river, evidently propelled with a vigour stimulated by fear. So great was the eagerness to cross that many trusted to a single plank as a means of support, and two small docks on the shore were completely stripped for this purpose."

On the night of June 2, Denison and the Body Guard were forced to sleep under the stars, as no provision had been made for providing food or shelter for the men. To Denison, it was another sign of government incompetence when it came to the military. He would later write,

> "The want of organization or preparation, in view of the long threatenings, seems almost incredible. I had to take my corps on a campaign without the carbines I had asked for, but with revolvers for which we had only some four or five ten-year-old paper cartridges for each. We did not know whether they would go off or not. We had no haversacks, no water-bottles, no nose bases (for the horses). Some of us had small tin cups fastened on our saddles. We had no canteens, or knives or forks, or cooking utensils of any kind or valises. We had no clothes except those on our backs. We had no tents and no blankets."

The next morning, the Body Guard moved to the front and discovered a scow loaded with Fenians in the middle of the Niagara River under what appeared to be the protection of the United States revenue cutter *Michigan*. The Fenians were still retreating, dumping their rifles as they went. The *Michigan* was simply standing by to arrest the Fenians once they reached shore on the U.S. side. As the Body Guard advanced down a road littered with Fenian guns, swords, and bayonets, the troopers captured a number of wounded Fenians who had been abandoned by their comrades in the woods.

For the next three weeks, Denison and the Body Guard

did outpost and patrol duties at Fort Erie. On June 20, with the danger passed, the entire force was ordered home. The Body Guard returned by the steamer *City of Toronto*, and marched through Toronto on the way to its barracks. Many of the men carried captured Fenian rifles and other war trophies — Denison reported that one even had a Fenian drum in front of his horse. The streets were crowded; on every side the volunteers were greeted with cheers and waving handkerchiefs. Denison and his men received the Canada General Service Medal with "Fenian Raid Bar 1866" as a reward for a job well done. And they deserved it — their force, consisting of only 55 mounted cavalry and three officers, had patrolled a frontier of 40 kilometres and kept in constant contact with headquarters 15 kilometres to the rear.

But Denison was bitter at the treatment the Body Guard had received from his superiors. Retiring to Heydon Villa and his law books, he continued to rail against the government, sometimes publicly, which did little to advance his position either politically or financially.

To raise some extra money, Denison once again turned to writing. In 1866, he had a paper titled "Fenian Raids at Fort Erie" and a book titled *Modern Cavalry* published. At that time, the military minds of Europe still saw a role for the cavalry charge (a mass of horses and men armed with swords and lances flying at the enemy). After all, the Charge of the Light Brigade — glorious disaster that it was — had occurred only a dozen years earlier and was the stuff of

G. T. Denison, seated centre, and officers, ca. 1895

legend throughout Europe.

Denison saw a less glamorous role for the mounted corps. Based on lessons learned during the American Civil War, he saw the cavalry becoming mounted infantry, riding to battle, dismounting at the front, and then fighting as infantry on foot. Denison's critics responded quickly — and in force. European military writers discounted him as a "colonial" who did not understand the real role of cavalry. They mocked his ideas and branded him as crazy. (It was not until after the start of World War I that the European establishment accepted the lessons that were learned during the American Civil War — and written about by the "crazy colonial colonel" 50 years earlier.)

By 1868, Denison had still not received his appointment — neither the nomination to the Conservative Party he had requested, nor the post of adjunct general for cavalry that Prime Minister MacDonald had proposed instead. Concluding that MacDonald would never award him either position, Denison resigned his commission as an officer in the Canadian militia.

* * *

As the years passed, there was one constant in Denison's life — he was always short of money. However, when he failed to win a seat in the provincial parliament in 1872, Sir Oliver Mowatt, premier of Ontario, offered him a patronage post as immigration commissioner in London, England. The money that came with the offer was a welcome change, and for Denison the posting was a chance to mix with the rich and famous in "the mother country."

But the patronage windfall was short-lived. In 1874, with his term position at an end, Denison returned to Toronto to an uncertain future. Reluctant to go back to practising law, he looked around for a more inspiring challenge.

Providence provided just the thing. The czar of Russia announced an international competition for the best book on the history of cavalry. The prize was a gold medal and 5000 roubles — a small fortune to Denison and a chance for the former cavalry officer to restore his place in Toronto society.

The contest posed three major problems for Denison. First, the czar demanded that the author be a serving cavalry officer, and Denison had resigned his commission. Second, the book needed to be translated to Russian, and there were no qualified translators in Canada. Finally, the book had to cover the entire history of cavalry, requiring research materials simply not available in 1870s Canada. Fortunately, he had nearly three years before his entry was due.

Denison first worked on regaining his commission. Swallowing his pride, he applied for and received the rank of major on May 5, 1874, commanding the second squadron of the Body Guard. His restored status as a serving cavalry officer made him eligible for the contest.

Closeted away at Heydon Villa and writing daily, Denison soon ran out of research materials. It was now 1876, leaving less than a year to complete his manuscript. To Denison, the solution was clear; he packed what he needed and moved to London, England. There, he continued his research and found an ex-patriot Russian to translate each chapter as he completed it.

True to form, Denison completed the book in early 1877 with time to spare. He was particularly proud that he had done what no British officer had even attempted. Indeed, his was the sole submission from the British Empire. Denison believed that more than just his personal fortune was at stake — to win would be a victory for both Canada and the empire, as well as a vindication for his ideas about the cavalry.

Before leaving to present *A History of Cavalry* to the czar and the judging committee, Denison met with several prominent Britons whom he knew from his time as immigration commissioner. They provided him with travel documents and letters of introduction to the Russian nobility.

Denison travelled to St. Petersburg on a diplomatic passport as a special emissary of the British government. But for all his preparations, his introduction to Russian society was hardly triumphant. He had intended to wear civilian clothes rather than his uniform when he made the presentation. However, upon his arrival he was told that he must wear a uniform. Not sure what to do, he asked for advice from the footman of one of the Russian nobles he was to meet. The footman took one look at the travel-weary Denison in his civilian clothes and turned him away.

After changing into his uniform, Denison left the hotel to present himself, and his book, to the Russian court. He must have made a better impression, because this time, the doorman arranged for a sleigh to bear Denison to his hosts.

Once again, nothing went according to plan. The czar's judging committee rejected Denison's book because "the translation was of such poor quality that it was unacceptable for the competition." Frustrated, but determined, Denison presented his letters of introduction to the Russians and persuaded them to provide him with new translators. Working day and night, often by candlelight, Denison and the translators completed the book again. Denison found it necessary to explain almost every phrase of the book to the translators. But he needn't have been so diligent. When he presented his book to the czar a second time, it was once again rejected — this time for missing the deadline. The medal and the glory slipped through Denison's grasp.

But if the fates had cursed Denison, they cursed his competitors still more; the Russian committee was so disappointed with the quality of the other submissions that they decided not to declare a winner. The czar announced that while Denison could not win the medal, having missed the deadline, he had nevertheless written the best book. Denison was awarded the 5000 rouble prize.

Though the money was welcome, it was a hollow victory for Denison. He acquired none of the prestige for which he had sacrificed so much. He felt that without the medal, neither he nor his work would be taken seriously by the British. And he was right. Denison returned to Canada dejected and disappointed, but not defeated. He later got the last laugh when *A History of Cavalry* became required reading for cavalry officers in all armies and cavalry schools across Europe — except England.

Upon his return to Canada, Denison was made a senior police magistrate in Toronto — a position he held until his death. He was known to deal with as many as 80 cases in a day and was usually finished work by noon. When city council complained that they were paying a full-time magistrate for a part-time job, Denison simply slowed down proceedings and clogged up the court. Council backed off.

The early 1880s were fine years for Denison. He felt financially secure enough to build a new Heydon Villa, a showplace complete with wide verandas and a widow's walk. He was politically active, writing more than ever, and he continued serving with his beloved Body Guard. He was finally settling into the role he always wanted — country gentleman and officer. But everything changed in February 1885 when his wife, Carrie, died. A few weeks later, Denison and the Body Guard were again called to battle.

The conflict involved a group of settlers along the South Saskatchewan River who were engaged in land disputes with the Canadian government. The people in the group were Métis, and their leader was Louis Riel.

When the government in Ottawa tried arbitrarily to change their land claims, the Métis rebelled. In March 1885, Riel established a provisional government, and the federal government ordered out the troops. The Riel Rebellion was to be the first military campaign conducted by the new Dominion with its own troops and at its own expense.

On March 30, the minister of the militia ordered the Governor General's Body Guard to active service, and by April 6, the corps was on a train headed west. Two days later, they reached the western end of the line at Dog Lake, where sections of the rail line were not yet completed. Time and time again the men and horses were unloaded, moved by land, and then reloaded onto trains for the next section of the line

— all in bitterly cold temperatures.

On the night of March 10, the Body Guard reached Magpie River Camp. The camp consisted of tents and a log shelter where the cavalry horses were stabled. After a midnight supper, the men tried to catch a little sleep by curling under blankets in their sleighs. They would need the rest — the trip to Winnipeg took nine days and covered over 2400 kilometres through biting cold and snow.

Major General Middleton, commanding officer of the Canadian Forces during the North-West Rebellion, ordered the Body Guard to protect the telegraph lines and trails used by military couriers to Winnipeg at Humboldt (Saskatchewan). Early on April 24, the corps left Winnipeg for Fort Qu'Appelle by train and then travelled on foot to Humboldt, reaching their destination on May 2. Upon their arrival they saw that teamsters, hired by Middleton, had delivered a large amount of military supplies by driving oxen carts across the prairies. Denison set to work protecting his camp and the supplies with a lightly built "fort."

Digging trenches and building fortifications was not work generally expected of cavalry. In fact, the corps only had six spades among them. Nevertheless, the Body Guard rallied to the task and, upon completion, the men decided to name their construction project "Fort Denison."

They didn't have long to enjoy their accomplishment. On May 18, troopers McNab and Simms, while out on a scouting party, captured a Sioux named Wahisea. Wahisea was a lieutenant to a Sioux chief named White Cap, who had participated with Sitting Bull at the Battle of the Little Big Horn — "the Custer Massacre." Chief White Cap and his band of Teton Sioux had found refuge in Canada and had agreed to settle on a reserve near Saskatoon. Under pressure from Riel and others, White Cap agreed to fight against the whites. His presence — with his band — had turned the tide at the Battle of Fish Creek, giving victory to Riel.

Under interrogation, Wahisea admitted that White Cap and his band were trying to escape from Canada and return to the United States. Denison immediately ordered Lieutenant Merritt to take a party of 25 men and try to capture White Cap and his followers. His instructions were "to press for a peaceful surrender; there was to be no fighting if it could possibly be avoided."

Taking Wahisea with them as a tracker, the Body Guard set out in search of White Cap. The band was moving south both day and night at such a pace that the Body Guard's horses began to fail. Merritt feared that if the Sioux were not caught soon the Body Guard would have to turn back.

At the end of the second day, the Body Guard caught up with the Sioux, who had stopped to graze their horses. Not believing that soldiers could travel as fast as they could, the Sioux had taken a moment of rest. The Body Guard approached cautiously, but when a Sioux warrior spotted them, he raised the alarm and White Cap's men ran for their rifles. To their surprise, however, the Body Guard held their fire. Merritt was determined to find a peaceful resolution, as Denison had instructed.

Evidently, White Cap felt the same way, because he ordered his followers to stand down. They agreed to return to Fort Denison under a flag of truce and surrender to Denison there. On the march back, at a more leisurely pace, the Body Guard calculated that they had chased the Sioux nearly 100 kilometres in a day and a half. It was the only time during the North-West Rebellion that a group of fugitive Native people were successfully tracked and captured.

White Cap was held at Fort Denison for a little over a month until General Middleton, feeling the chief was no longer a military threat, ordered his release. But if he was no longer of significance to the military, the North-West Mounted Police felt differently—White Cap was still a wanted outlaw. The NWMP brought him to Regina in chains to stand trial. But the Canadian minister of justice, eager to dispense with the whole affair, ordered him released and he returned to his reserve.

With hostilities ended, the Body Guard left Humboldt on July 9, finally reaching Toronto on July 23. Despite Denison's disappointment with their role, the Body Guard earned its first battle honour — The North-West Rebellion 1885 — and he and his men each received the North-West Canada Medal.

The North-West Rebellion came to an official end on July 2, 1885, after Middleton and his forces drove the rebels from Manitoba and captured Louis Riel. Convicted of treason, Riel would later be hanged.

* * *

On his return to Toronto, Denison resumed both his military and public service duties. On December 1, 1887, he married the second Mrs. Denison, Helen Amanda Mair. In 1889, he was appointed lieutenant colonel, commanding, of the Governor General's Body Guard of Ontario, and was still in command when the regiment's name was officially changed to the Governor General's Body Guard in 1895, recognizing that Canada was now a unified country and there was need for only one official Body Guard.

After years of service — and to make room for a younger generation — Colonel G.T. Denison III was placed on the reserve officers list in 1898 and ultimately accepted the position of honorary lieutenant colonel of the regiment in 1899.

Though Denison's military battles had come to an end, his political battles were far from over. Denison had always been a champion of Britain and the concept of a unified empire. He was also vehemently anti-American. Thus, when a Canadian investor proposed a "Commercial Union" between Canada and the United States, Denison took umbrage.

The investor was one Erastus Wiman, a Canadian working in the United States. Wiman, along with many other businessmen, believed the Commercial Union would strengthen the economy and political standing of the new Dominion.

During the summer of 1887, he held meetings and lobbied Parliament to support the plan.

The proposal seemed to be gaining acceptance in Ottawa — until it landed in the sights of George Denison III. Denison believed the Commercial Union would bring about the annexation of Canada — indeed, he believed Wiman had designed the proposal for that very purpose.

To counter the plan, Denison lit upon an obscure movement begun in England in 1884. The "Imperial Federation League" wished to secure an Imperial Federation using the Canadian Confederation as a model. When he first heard of the group, Denison was unimpressed — they were small and their cause seemed to lack a *raison d'être*. At the time, the relationship between Canada and the rest of the British Empire was never better, and the United States seemed preoccupied with its own rebuilding effort after the Civil War.

Three years later, however, the Imperial Federation League seemed to Denison like the perfect foil to Wiman's Commercial Union with the United States. Far beyond simply championing the league's cause, Denison became its president in 1893. He directed his considerable energy at promoting a stronger vision of empire in order to supplant any union with the Americans. To Denison, the Dominion's very identity was at stake: "By advocating Imperial Federation it enabled us to appeal to the old dream of the United Empire Loyalists of the Revolution. It gave the opportunity of appealing to our history, to the sacrifices of our fathers, to all the traditions of race, and the ties of blood and kindred, to the sacrifices and the victories of the war of 1812, and to the national spirit of our people, to preserve our status as a part of the British Empire."

Even when the threat of a Commercial Union was long gone and the Americans had made it clear they were not interested in annexing Canada, Denison continued to publicly advocate "a trade policy between Great Britain and her Colonies by means of which a discrimination in the exchange of natural and manufactured products will be made in favour of one another, and against foreign nations."

While there was never a formal trade pact between England and Canada, Denison's anti-Americanism just would not die. In 1902, he wrote his defence of a united empire in a work entitled *Struggle for Imperial Unity*, which was really his political memoirs.

For the next 20 years, Denison occupied himself in his role as police magistrate, continuing to see cases at a sensational rate. He published his final book, *Recollections of a Police Magistrate*, in 1920. With over 650,000 cases tried in his court, Denison claimed to have handled more criminal cases in his career than any other magistrate in the British Empire — who was going to argue?

When the colonel finally passed away on June 6, 1925, newspaper headlines simply read, "Denison Dead." No other explanation was necessary — every Canadian knew that an era of their political and military history had come to an end.

Chapter 3

Major General Sir Henry Mill Pellatt and the Queen's Own Rifles

enry Mill Pellatt was born in Kingston, Ontario, on January 6, 1859, to Henry Pellatt Sr. and Emma Mary Holland — both originally from England. Ambitious from the very beginning, Henry Jr. embraced the spirit of the family motto: *Devant Si Je Puis,* or "Foremost If I Can."

As a young man, Pellatt achieved a great deal in just a few years. At 17, he left the prestigious Upper Canada College to join his father's stock brokerage firm, Pellatt and Osler.

With his career off to a flying start, the making of Henry Pellatt, the legend, wasn't far behind. At 19, he entered the North American Champion Mile Race in New York City, and won. Pellatt beat the U.S. amateur running champion and finished the final 100 metres in just 12 seconds — a feat that remained unmatched until 1930.

Pellatt was only 20 when he met Mary Dodgson, a local girl, and fell in love. He knew he could not ask Mary to be his wife until he was financially stable, so when he was 23, he became a full partner in the brokerage firm, changing the name to Pellatt and Pellatt. That same year, with their financial future now secure, Henry and Mary wed.

Even in his early 20s, Pellatt had a gift for spotting revolutionary ideas. When Thomas Edison developed a practical method to produce steam-generated electricity in 1883, Pellatt realized that supplying electricity to homes and businesses could be lucrative. That same year, he raised the capital necessary to found the Toronto Electric Light Company, named himself corporate secretary, and paid himself the grand sum of $25 per month. Pellatt soon had his first contract with the city to install 32 arc lights in downtown Toronto.

By the time Pellatt was 30, the Toronto Electric Light Company was the only company authorized to provide street lighting — a 30-year monopoly granted by the city fathers. In addition to power, the company generated enormous wealth for the Pellatts until 1910. That year, against Pellatt's most vehement protests, the Ontario government nationalized electric production. Pellatt was forced to sell his electric company to the publicly owned Hydro Electric Power Commission of Ontario — an affront he never got over.

In 1892, Pellatt's father retired (rumours swirled through

Toronto society that his son paid him to leave the firm), enabling Henry Jr. to take more risks in his investing. In fact, he acquired the nickname "Pellatt the Plunger" for his reputation for recklessness in the stock market. More experienced investors were focussing on companies in Eastern Canada — they were solid and safe. Pellatt was unconvinced, focussing instead on the Canadian Pacific Railway (CPR) and the North West Land Company. He became known in Canadian financial circles as the only man who would buy North West Land stock at any price. He gathered up, and held, the stock at $12 and $14 a share, even as others were selling the shares as fast as they could.

Pellatt was betting on the West — he believed a flood of immigrants to the Prairies would create a demand for rail travel and land on which to settle. His intuition proved correct: a liberal immigration policy led to the opening of the Canadian West, and the CPR and North West Land reaped enormous profits. The North West venture alone created over four million dollars in profits for investors in Pellatt and Pellatt — and for Henry Pellatt Jr. personally.

By 1901, his portfolio included interests in mining, insurance, land, and electricity, and Pellatt himself was chairing the boards of 21 companies. These companies were a who's who of Canadian business, and included the Dominion Iron and Steel Company, the Crows Nest Coal Company, the Brazilian Traction Company, the Toronto Railway Company, Page Hersey Tubes Limited, the Richelieu and Ontario

Navigation Company, the Twin City Rapid Transit Company, McIntyre Mines Limited, the Mining Corporation of Canada, the British American Assurance Company, the Western Assurance Company, and many others. In 1903, Pellatt and his partners were building the first Canadian hydro-generating plant, having won the rights to harness the waters at Niagara Falls.

By now, Pellatt was well known to Canadians. Everyone knew he was rich beyond most peoples' dreams and that he was one of Canada's most powerful men. Yet rather than resenting him, the public found him fascinating. Whatever he did made the papers.

In 1907, a Canadian publication asked the financier for the keys to his success. Pellatt replied, "Never invest a cent of your own money in any proposition without a most careful investigation; never give any advice when asked unless your knowledge is sufficiently complete to do so intelligently; always have the courage of your convictions; never permit your expenses to go over 60 percent of your income; never allow over indulgence in any pleasure to get the best of your thinking powers; always judge your associates as you find them, at the same time carefully noting anything you may hear to the contrary; and at last but no means least, always respect your parents and relatives and never refuse to extend the helping hand, if you can afford it, to deserving mankind."

The Pellatts used their wealth to support a number of philanthropic projects, from endowments to universities and museums, to the development of major hospital installations, to large donations for the arts.

Pellatt's public profile and his philanthropy were rewarded when two governor generals, Earl Grey (1904–1911) and His Royal Highness the Duke of Connaught (1911–1916), appointed him honorary aide de camp (ADC) during their terms in Canada. Pellatt, in return, gratefully supported the monarchy and its Canadian representatives. When the Duke and Duchess of Cornwall and York (later King George V and Queen Mary) visited Toronto in 1901, Pellatt arranged to have 11,000 militia members parade in their honour, and he even loaned his personal horse to the duke. Patriotism only went so far, though. When the future king offered to buy the horse, Pellatt turned him down.

In 1905, Pellatt was knighted. In later years, he would publicly state that his knighthood was for his work in bringing the first electric power from Niagara. However, when Governor General Grey wrote to the king recommending Pellatt for the honour, there was no mention of electricity. Instead, the governor general went to great lengths to point out the sums of money Pellatt had spent in support of the military and the monarchy.

* * *

Pellatt's commitment to the military was life-long. Like his financial career, his military career began at the age of 17.

Before leaving college, he became part of the school's cadet corps, the Upper Canada College Rifle Company, the 11th Company of the Queen's Own Rifles. On November 2, 1876, he joined up as a common rifleman in Company F.

The Queen's Own Rifles had a long and glorious history. Canada's second oldest militia regiment, the officers and soldiers were expected to return their pay to the regiment to cover expenses. The privilege of serving in such an elite military unit was considered reward enough.

And elite it was — during the Fenian Raids of 1866 and the Riel Rebellion of 1870, the then Volunteer Militia Rifles of Canada had served with distinction.

Young Pellatt had been determined to hold up his end in the outfit, so he'd hired an experienced officer to train him in the intricacies of drilling. In the Pellatt home, Henry's instructor used matches to represent various military units and engagements, concentrating on the great battles of history until the young private "became more than a match for the officer."

Pellatt continued to apply himself in his military role, ever ready to answer the call of Queen and Country. That call came in 1877, when Pellatt participated in his one and only real battle, the Grand Trunk Railway strike in Belleville, Ontario.

At the time, railways were steadily emerging as a vital link across both Quebec and Ontario, allowing people and goods to move around that rapidly expanding region. The arrival of the Grand Trunk Railway in 1856 gave Belleville a commercial link with Canada's largest economic centres, Montreal and Toronto. In addition to making the little town a major regional trading centre, railway headquarters were in Belleville, making it the area's largest employer.

However, by 1876 a severe recession had gripped not just Belleville, but all of the Dominion. The Grand Trunk Railway was soon facing financial difficulties. Just before Christmas, the company laid off 66 engineers in order to save the three dollars a day they were being paid. Other engineers working for the railway immediately walked off the job and declared a strike. The walkout caught everyone by surprise, including a train full of passengers stranded in Belleville in the middle of a snowstorm. The strikers made newspaper headlines across the country as the demonstrations escalated into a five-day riot.

Armed with whatever they could find, including a few pistols, strikers and sympathizers alike showed up at the Grand Trunk station in Belleville threatening violence. The small police force, not prepared to deal with the large and angry crowd, quickly retreated and called in a detachment of the 49th Regiment to restore order.

Not deterred by the show of force, the mob grew larger and larger, and soon a call went out for another 40 men from the 15th Battalion, but they, too, failed in the face of the hostile strikers. The mayor of Belleville, realizing the riot had grown so out of hand that local forces could not contain it alone, called on Ottawa to provide military support.

On January 2, 1877, Pellatt answered a knock at his front door. A winded messenger urgently explained that Pellatt and 167 other men and officers of the Queen's Own Rifles were to report immediately to the "Old Fort" in Toronto, ready for active duty. Pellatt had a good idea what it was all about — he had been following the railway strikes in the local papers.

Within hours, Pellatt and the Queen's Own were on a train headed for Belleville. The soldiers had some cause for anxiety; the officers of the Queen's Own had explained that there had been threats of violence against the officials of the Grand Trunk Railway, and even against the regiment's own troop train.

As the train moved towards Belleville, the weather began to worsen. Snow, driven by a strong wind, reduced visibility to almost nothing. Tensions continued to grow as the officers of the Queen's Own ordered men to ride at the front of the engine and outside the cars to watch for strikers. Pellatt took his turn at guard duty, which included standing on train platforms in the bitter cold whenever the train stopped at stations for water and coal.

The officers ordered the train to stop a short distance outside of Belleville, wary of what might await them. For three days the strikers had been pummelling the railroad with stones, bricks, and insults; the appearance of the Queen's Own would give the strikers a new target and a revived sense of outrage. The regiment formed up and marched towards downtown Belleville and their first target — the train station. As the men approached, the mob of unemployed workers and their supporters hurled stones, bricks, and bolts that had been ripped from railroad machinery.

Pellatt and his comrades advanced up the street, shoulder to shoulder with their rifles slung on their backs, trying not to provoke the crowd. But the hail of stones and bolts continued unabated. Within moments, two of the Queen's Own were knocked down and severely injured. In the face of escalating violence, the officers of the regiment ordered their men to fix bayonets.

Unslinging his Snider Enfield, Pellatt locked the bayonet into place. On order, he and 160 other troops of the Queen's Own levelled their weapons at the crowd. The troops advanced — no easy task on the ice-covered streets of Belleville in January. Slowly, inch by inch, the crowd was driven back at the point of the bayonets. A number of the strikers were injured as the troops took back the streets.

Over the next two days, Pellatt and the other Queen's Own soldiers regained control of the town using the train station as their centre of operations. On January 3, the regiment was relieved and they returned to Toronto. For the rest of his career, Pellatt proudly wore his official battle medal, which was made from the steel of melted-down railway tracks.

Pellet's future "battles" were more controlled, and definitely less messy. In 1897, Queen Victoria was celebrating 60 years on the throne, and the Canadian government decided to send a delegation to mark the occasion. Ottawa agreed that the militia would contribute a composite group of 300 soldiers — including those from the Queen's Own Rifles. Major Henry Pellatt made sure he was one of the officers.

When the Canadians arrived in England, they were a small part of an imperial "army" of over 25,000 men from India, Africa, Australia, and New Zealand. For his part, Major Pellatt could not have been more proud as he marched past the reviewing stand and saluted Queen Victoria.

Pellatt was tapped for an additional privilege — he commanded the guard of honour at the Thanksgiving mass at St. Paul's Cathedral. Until his death, he treasured the signed photograph of Queen Victoria that he received as a thank-you for his service.

Although the trip was a great personal success for Pellatt, the experience nevertheless upset him deeply because he felt that the Queen's Own Rifles were not treated with the dignity and respect they deserved. On his return to Canada, he pointed out that the Rifles had even been forced to go out and buy their own food and provisions while they were in England. It is not clear whether Pellatt blamed the Canadian or British governments for this, but he swore he would never again place his men in the same embarrassing position.

In 1901, Pellatt was named the commanding officer of the Queen's Own Rifles, and was soon on his way back to England. This time he was commanding the Canadian contingent to the coronation of Edward VII in 1902. The

Canadians, all 657 of them, were to join 2000 other colonials at the Alexandra Palace to begin preparations for the coronation. On June 16, Pellatt met with the Duke of Connaught, who was to have overall command.

Pellatt and the Canadians were concerned. The camp was rife with rumours that Edward was too sick for the coronation to go ahead. On June 24, the worst was confirmed. The future king needed immediate surgery if his life was to be saved. As the Queen's Own Rifles were volunteers, they could not wait indefinitely for the coronation and returned to Canada. For Pellatt, it was a great opportunity lost, but he did send the Queen's Own bugle band to the actual coronation later that summer.

In 1906, at the invitation of the 12th Regiment of New York, Pellatt went to New York City with 900 officers and men of the Queen's Own. The regiment put on a display of military manoeuvres that was so well received that Pellatt was promoted to colonel. Once again, he landed on the front pages back home.

Sir Henry Pellatt was as generous in military matters as he was to civilian charities. His largesse ran from hosting regular mess dinners for the regiment, to holding a lavish celebration in honour of the 50th anniversary of the Queen's Own Rifles. In June 1910, the Pellatts hosted a weeklong celebration to showcase themselves and Canada's history. The family entertained over 10,000 Torontonians by hosting nightly two-hour-long performances that featured 1200 people, two military bands, pipers, and 400 schoolchildren. The performances were so large and complicated that when John Thorn died during the re-enactment of the Battle of Queenston Heights, his death went almost unnoticed.

Celebrations aside, Pellatt conferred with Lord Roberts, the regiment's honorary colonel, regarding a visit to England by the Queen's Own Rifles. The two agreed that such a visit would show imperial unity at a time when European sabre rattling was growing louder. Pellatt, in his role as aide de camp, had quietly discussed the possibility of a visit to England with the governor general as early as 1909. It was reported that when King Edward heard of Pellatt's plan he gave it his unqualified support, sending a telegraph that read, "Cable them to come at once."

So, Pellatt and the Queen's Own Rifles prepared to depart for England to take part in the British Army's seven-week-long autumn manoeuvres at Aldershot. The Canadian government warned Sir Henry that there was no money for such an extravagance. His reply? He would pay the entire cost himself.

Even the *Toronto World* newspaper — which had often been critical of Sir Henry Pellatt — was forced to admit it was a hugely generous offer: "In money cost alone it will approach if not exceed a quarter of a million dollars — but even that expenditure does not measure its importance ... No act of any single man could bring the United Kingdom into closer touch with her daughter states than this splendid act of Sir Henry

Pellatt. Without it he ranked among the most enthusiastic and capable of militia officers within the British Empire — its achievement will make him the most distinguished."

On August 15, 1910, 632 officers and men were at the Toronto drill shed, ready to board two Grand Trunk Railway trains for the trip to Montreal. After a period of intense training in Quebec, the regiment sailed for Britain aboard the SS *Megantic.* Among their fellow passengers was the infamous Dr. Crippen, returning to England under guard to stand trial for murdering his wife. Crippen stayed well under cover during the trip, but when the Queen's Own landed in England, they found they had acquired a grim nickname: "Crippen's Own."

The trip to Aldershot was probably one of the most extensively covered "events" of the decade. Six official reporters, including five who were in their militia uniforms, were assigned by their various newspapers to cover the journey — and tagging along for the fun of it were many more unofficial reporters. The first "major event" the reporters covered onboard the *Megantic* was a tug of war between the officers and the sergeants of the regiment. General consensus was that the officers won only because their anchorman was Colonel Pellatt himself, all 300 pounds of him pulling with all his might.

"The Overseas Battalion" arrived at Liverpool on August 27, and was soon at Aldershot, ready to begin a new cycle of training and preparation. As hard as the training was, it was a disease, typhoid, that would cause the most difficulties for the Queen's Own. Six officers became ill, and Lieutenant R.M. Gzowski passed away from its effects. Buried in the Aldershot Military Cemetery, he was the first Queen's Own to die on overseas service.

From September 5 to 13, the Queen's Own, together with a battalion of British troops, the Leicester Buffs, were involved in a series of extensive and difficult military manoeuvres. The two units were soon so close on both military and personal levels that they became officially affiliated. During the final mock battle, umpires ruled that the Queen's Own had officially "wiped out half" of the East Yorkshire Regiment, and they were declared the winners. Altogether, England spent well over one million dollars on the two weeks of manoeuvres — partly to cover the costs of introducing the latest military inventions, including the aeroplane.

With World War I on the horizon, England was glad for the show of Canadian support — even if privately funded. In the end, Pellatt spent over $150,000 of his own money to attend the manoeuvres. By late September, it was time for the Queen's Own Rifles to head home. In London, the lord mayor hosted a farewell dinner for the regiment at Guild Hall. Before departing, Pellatt attended one last ceremony, at Balmoral Castle, where King George V presented him with the "Commander of the Victorian Order." He was now Sir Henry Pellatt, CVO.

Pellatt returned home inspired by the grandness of

Europe. Enamoured with the architecture he had seen in his travels, he hired Canadian architect E.J. Lennox to help him lay out the plans for a Scottish Baronial castle overlooking Toronto. His first step was to purchase 25 acres of land that had been called *Casa Loma*, or "house on the hill," by its previous owner.

Pellatt's Casa Loma took three years and over $3.5 million to build. Pellatt had always known he would one day have a castle of his own. While travelling through Europe, he had collected drawings and photos of other castles, all of which he gave to Lennox for inspiration. The architect built Pellatt's castle on massive foundations to support thick stone walls, soaring towers, and 98 rooms. Hoping that Casa Loma would one day become a military and historical museum, Pellatt insisted that the main floor be strong enough to hold displays of heavy military equipment. Lennox complied and built them from reinforced concrete covered in teak.

Casa Loma's basement was large enough to allow a full regiment to stay the night. Moreover, the castle's kitchen oven could roast a whole cow at one time to feed the visiting soldiers, and a rifle range was provided so that the Queen's Own Rifles never missed target practice. The gardens and lawns surrounding the house were designed to host full-scale military parades — and often did.

Sir Henry, when not at the offices of Pellatt and Pellatt, was often found in his study behind a desk that was an exact replica of Napoleon's. Surrounded by walls panelled

Casa Loma—residence of Sir Henry Pellatt.

in Spanish mahogany and featuring a hand-sculpted Italian marble fireplace, the study was his personal retreat. It had a secret staircase on either side of the fireplace — one led to the second floor, the other to Pellatt's private vault.

After 36 years of militia service, Sir Henry resigned as commanding officer of the Queen's Own Rifles in 1912. He had been the regiment's commanding officer for just over

11 years. However, his military service was not over. The Canadian government asked him to take over the command of the 6th Infantry Division. The division existed mostly in name, but it allowed Pellatt to be promoted to the rank of major general.

Regardless of his new position, Pellatt's legacy with the Queen's Own Rifles was assured. During World War I, his old regiment sent 210 officers and 7352 volunteers to serve in France and Flanders. On the battlefields of Ypres, the Somme, and Vimy Ridge, the Queen's Own stood out as some of Canada's best soldiers. Many were captured, and Pellatt established an organization to send food and clothing to members of the Queen's Own Rifles who were being held as prisoners of war. Further, as the commissioner of the Federal Military Hospital Commission, he ensured that the hospitalized soldiers in Canada received the best possible care and treatment.

For the most part, Pellatt's touch had been golden during his career. However, not even Pellatt the Plunger could have foreseen the impact of World War I. During the war, even as Sir Henry was made a brigadier general, Canadians patriotically put their money into war bonds, not the stock market. After the war, the Canadian economy plunged into a recession that ultimately forced Pellatt and Pellatt out of business. The company defaulted on loans owed to the Home Bank of Canada totalling $1.7 million (and over 10 times that amount in today's dollars).

The collapse of Pellatt and Pellatt caused the bankruptcy of the Home Bank in 1923 — the last Canadian bank bankruptcy until the Principal Group in Alberta in 1987. The Home Bank fallout was both financial and personal. When the smoke finally cleared, it was evident that the cost had been extremely high: five people had died, Prime Minister William Lyon Mackenzie King had been forced to appear at public hearings to explain his government's lack of response to the crisis, and two bank officers and six directors, as well as Ontario's provincial treasurer, had been sent to jail. In the end, the depositors — about 60,000 of them — received 60 cents on the dollar for their deposits due to a cash infusion of five million dollars from the federal government.

With his company bankrupt and his personal holdings almost worthless, the worst was yet to come for Pellatt. The City of Toronto and its tax assessors dealt him an extraordinarily high tax bill — unfairly high, he would continue to insist. As a result of all these blows, he had no choice but to auction off his prized possessions for pennies on the dollar and abandon his beloved Casa Loma. In all, the final auction of Pellatt's collection earned only $140,000 — a far cry from the $3.5 million it was rumoured to have cost. The Pellatts had lived in their castle for just over 10 years.

In 1924, after leaving Casa Loma, Sir Henry and Lady Pellatt moved to their 1000-acre Lake Marie farm in King Township. The farm was really a country estate, complete with cut-stone buildings and an old log cabin dating back to

L-R: Lieutenant General Sir William Dillon Otter,
Major General Sir Henry Pellatt,
Major General Robert Rennie.

the 1840s. Lady Pellatt, weakened by the strain of the move and the financial difficulties, passed away later that year at the age of 67.

Despite his many personal losses, Pellatt never lost his

sense of generosity or his love of grand spectacle. In 1926, his golden anniversary of service with the Queen's Own Rifles was celebrated with friends and the regiment, which was then being commanded by his son, Colonel Reg Pellatt, DSO (Distinguished Service Order, awarded for meritorious service). A detachment of the Leicester Buffs, out of respect for the long relationship between the two regiments, came from England. Pellatt, the Buffs, and Colonel Harry Cockshutt, the lieutenant governor of Ontario, took the salute as 500 men marched past.

The Queen's Own always saw Pellatt as their champion — no matter how shaky the future might be. To show their respect for the old general, the men presented him with a ceremonial sword during the golden anniversary celebration. Then the nursing order of St. John of Jerusalem, an organization that had always benefited from Pellatt's generosity, gave him a long service medal, and the National Chorus presented him with a silver salver in recognition of his support of community music. The day ended with three airplanes from Camp Borden honouring the general with a fly-by.

In 1927, Pellatt once again married. Sir Henry and Catherine Merritt of St. Catharines, Ontario, spent their time entertaining, but their happiness was short-lived. Just before Christmas 1929, the second Lady Pellatt died of cancer.

Ten years later, the Royal York Hotel in Toronto was the scene of the final mess dinner for the "Aldershot Boys." On January 6, 1939, 225 of the men Pellatt had taken to England gathered to celebrate his 80th birthday. Long past his glory days of financial and social power, the general enjoyed the company of the men he admired most, the Queen's Own. Queen Mary, out of respect for Pellatt's support and friendship, sent a letter of congratulations.

Sir Henry Pellatt died just two months later, on March 8, 1939. The general's casket, topped by the Union Jack and his hat and presentation sword, was borne on a horse-drawn carriage through the streets of Toronto. Citizens lined the streets to pay their last respects. They watched as 350 members of the Queen's Own Rifles marched past, led by the regimental sergeant major carrying Pellatt's 12 medals and decorations on a purple pillow. A riderless stallion followed the casket as the Queen's Own band played a funeral dirge. At the Forest Lawn Mausoleum, a volley of shots was fired as the Last Post was played. Sir Henry would have loved the pomp and circumstance.

Chapter 4

Joe Boyle and the Yukon Motor Machine Gun Brigade

oseph W. Boyle was no average Canadian. In a country whose motto is "Peace, Order and Good Government," Joe himself embodied the opposite; he liked a good fight, courted chaos, and was governed more by passion than by reason. Maybe Canada wasn't big enough to hold a deck hand, boxing promoter, millionaire mine owner, soldier, and lover to the Romania Queen all rolled into one. Klondike Joe Boyle didn't think so, at any rate.

Joe was born in Toronto on November 16, 1867, to Charles and Martha Boyle. He was the second youngest of four children, with two older brothers, Charles Jr. and Dave, and a sister, Susan. Joe's father was a wealthy racehorse breeder with many successful horses, including at least one Queen's Plate winner, to his credit. In 1872, Charles moved his family to Woodstock, Ontario, where Joe and his siblings led an idyllic existence riding horses, boating, swimming, and fishing.

Like most children in Woodstock, Joe attended public school and then, after graduation in 1882, entered Woodstock College. Upon graduating in 1884, Joe told his father that he wanted to work in the horseracing business, but Charles would have none of it. Had Charles known of the dangers and adventures Joe would go on to face, he might have made a different decision.

Recognizing that his father would not change his mind, Joe left Woodstock and joined his two brothers, Charlie and Dave, in New York City. At 17, he decided to live the dream of many boys, a dream that few had the courage to pursue. One day, Joe headed for the docks, and the romance of the sailing ships moored there. He quickly found a ship's captain and told him about his desire to live a life of adventure. The captain immediately took the young Canadian under his wing, hiring him as a deck hand on the *Wailace*.

It was only after Joe had signed on that he found out the ship was leaving in two hours. When he got home, he found the house empty and, not wanting to miss his chance at adventure, left a simple note that read: "I've gone to sea. Please don't worry about me. –Joe."

Joe was nothing if not independent. For the next three years, as he travelled the world, he did not send his family a single letter. He laid the groundwork for a bigger-than-life image early. A story that may or may not have been true quickly spread through the ranks of sailors in the ports that Joe visited. According to the story, Joe, armed with only a knife, had jumped overboard to successfully rescue a shipmate from an attacking shark. He had apparently driven the beast away by repeatedly stabbing it in the nose.

The *Wailace* sailed back to New York and stopped in Nova Scotia for provisions. There, the captain released Joe from his contract, and Joe immediately shipped out on another vessel. But luck seemed to elude him; the ship went aground near Cork, Ireland, forcing Joe to work as a tour guide until he found another ship willing to hire him.

When Joe finally returned to New York in 1887, his brother Dave threw a party in his honour and, at the same time, introduced him to Mildred Raynor. Three days later, Joe and the attractive divorcée were married. Not long after their wedding, the first of their seven children was born. (As was normal for the time, only four of their children actually survived to adulthood.)

Joe soon established a small animal feed business serving the horseracing world he knew through his father. Though he was now moderately wealthy, his wanderlust quickly had him looking for more adventures. While managing a boxing club in 1897, he met professional heavyweight boxer Frank Slavin (the "Sydney Slasher"). The two became friends and were soon setting up fights across the Dominion and the United States.

By 1896, Joe's marriage was in trouble and the Boyles separated. Joe returned to Canada accompanied by his eldest children, Joseph Jr. and Flora, while Mildred stayed in New York with their other daughter and unborn child. Soon, Joe and the two children were living back at his family's farm, "The Firs," in Woodstock.

Joe was soon overtaken with wanderlust, and while he and Frank were away promoting boxing matches in San Francisco, they heard rumours about fields of gold in the Klondike that were just waiting for adventurers like them. Leaving his two children with his parents, Joe, together with Frank, literally fought his way to the Klondike — both men took turns in the ring. Staging boxing tournaments to finance their journey to the Yukon, the two partners saved just enough money to pay their way to Skagway, Alaska. There, they joined a party of miners and took the long, treacherous path over the White Pass Route to Dawson City.

Though the two fight promoters had dreams of staking their own claims on the Klondike, they arrived there with just $22 between them. As a result, both men were forced to work at the Eldorado 13 claim, owned by the famous Swiftwater Bill Gates. A wanderer from Idaho, Swiftwater Bill had been working as a dishwasher in the North when he joined the gold rush in the Klondike. At Eldorado 13, he and his prospecting partners had sunk seven shafts into the river gravel before hitting pay dirt. Then suddenly, the lowly dishwasher became a tycoon.

Joe and Frank, on the other hand, were grunts, breaking their backs panning for gold in the icy rivers. Joe figured there had to be a better way to profit from all the wealth just lying in the Klondike and its tributaries. He believed that dredging (using mechanical machines to dig the gold from the rivers) was the way to his fortune.

In the summer of 1897, Joe and Frank did what they could to ensure their future. The two men registered claims covering over 10,000 hectares, stretching along 13 kilometres of river. That fall, Frank stayed in the Yukon to file their claims while Joe, travelling with Swiftwater Bill, headed to Ottawa to arrange for the licences required to dredge in the Klondike River Valley.

It was a difficult trip. With little equipment, not even a tent, they traversed the snow-covered passes by day and slept in the open at night. One month after leaving the gold fields, they arrived in Seattle. Dredging proposals in hand, Joe then made for Ottawa by train.

In Ottawa, Joe met with Clifford Sifton, Canadian Minister of the Interior. Sifton made it clear that he believed "Canadians should be developing — and profiting from —the Klondike gold fields." Joe left the nation's capital with Sifton's assurance that the licences would be fairly considered.

Upon his return to the Yukon, Joe was amazed at how much Dawson City had grown. Thousands of would-be miners, and the usual camp hangers-on, were settling in the Yukon Territory.

Recognizing an opportunity when he saw one, Joe built a sawmill to provide timber to the miners, who needed it for building their cabins, furniture, sluice boxes, and other mining apparatus. Cut timber was almost worth its weight in gold, and the money was pouring in. Joe expanded by building a storehouse, wharf, and lumber dock. He also acquired 17 more mining claims and constructed a large cabin along Bear Creek to serve as his headquarters for the Bear Creek Company.

Timber was a brisk business, but Joe knew the real prize was gold. He found a wealthy investor to finance the cost of machinery, and the Bear Creek Company soon became the Canadian Klondike Mining Company. Between his lumber and mining operations, Joe was well on his way to amassing a fortune — and he was determined to put it to good use.

Ahead of his time as always, Joe wanted the same thing that many of today's tycoons want: a sports team. He managed and financed the Dawson Nuggets, a hockey team made up of Klondike prospectors and civil servants. In 1905, the Nuggets took on the Stanley Cup Challenge. They were to play against the "invincible" Ottawa Silver Seven. Paying for the $6000 trip out of his own fortune, Joe led the team on a 6500-kilometre journey that included walking, dogsledding, bicycling, and riding the Canadian Pacific Railway. The team of Yukoners, despite attempting to stay in condition on the train by jumping rope in the smoking car, arrived in Ottawa tired and horribly out of shape.

The next day, Friday the 13th, the Ottawa Silver Seven beat the Dawson Nuggets 9-2 as Governor General Earl Grey looked on. As disappointed as the Klondike team was with this first game, it turned out much better than the next game, when Ottawa won 23-2. It was not just the score that was humiliating — 14 of Ottawa's points were scored by Frank McGee, Ottawa's star center, who had only one eye. A reported for the *Toronto Telegram* later wrote that the Nuggets were the "worst consignment of hockey junk to come over the metals of the CPR."

In 1909, while in Ontario, Joe married Elma Louise Humphries. Joe and Elma were happy enough, but his daughter from his first marriage fought with her stepmother at every turn. Joe, thinking a new house would bring domestic peace, returned to the Yukon with Elma and Flora.

The Canadian Klondike Mining Company continued to grow, and Joe's brother Charlie, with a new bride and a small son, soon joined him in the Yukon. Joe and Charlie got to work planning a 'dreadnought dredge'. The brothers' newest project would be the largest dredge in the world, handling 11,000 cubic meters worth of sludge and gravel a day. In 1910, the dredge, christened the *Canadian*, finally began to work — and immediately added to Joe's wealth.

With the *Canadian* operating at maximum capacity, Joe began to make plans to build two more super dredges. The first dredge began operation in 1913, and one year later the second dredge joined it in service. Together, Joe's dredges were mining more gravel than eight regular dredges on any other claim in the Klondike.

By 1914, Joe was looking for new challenges. Though the company was doing well, the *Canadian* mysteriously sank, and Joe's power plant and laundromat were damaged by fire. Joe found that running a company was not as much fun as building one.

His next great challenge came when Archduke Ferdinand was assassinated in Sarajevo and Canada declared that, in support of Great Britain, it was now at war with Germany. When Joe heard of the war in Europe, he immediately tried to volunteer to serve in the Canadian Expeditionary Force. However, he was too well known — and too wealthy — to be a simple private. And, with his chequered past, there was not much chance he would be made an officer. In fact, the Canadian government made it clear that there would be no active service role for Joe.

Meanwhile, Canada's minister of militia and defence, Sir Sam Hughes, recognized that the Canadian Army did not have the equipment it needed, or the money to pay for it. He spread the word that the government would gratefully accept any contributions from private citizens.

Joe immediately decided to use his own fortune to organize a unit that would become known as the "Yukon Boys." All volunteers, the men were equipped with machine guns and given uniforms of khaki trousers, woollen shirts, yellow mackinaws, and stiff-brimmed sombreros. Joe personally designed the Yukon Boys' cap badge, which featured crossed machine guns on a miner's pan, topped with the initials "YT" (Yukon Territory).

Once the group was assembled, Joe wrote to Hughes, offering the Yukon Boys — a 50-man, machine-gun detachment — to the Dominion for active service. On September 4, 1914, Hughes accepted the offer. Joe had originally intended that his Boys would be a dashing artillery unit with purebred horses racing the fast firing guns to the front. But even to the romantic Joe, it quickly became evident that automobiles would replace horses in this war. So, he decided that the new unit would be equipped with armoured motor cars, and that it would be called the Yukon Motor Machine Gun Battery.

Two Royal North-West Mounted Police (RNWMP) officers were pressed into duty to give the Machine Gun Battery its basic training. Joe, impatient to get into battle, took the battery to Victoria, continuing to pay their wages and expenses. The Canadian government, finally taking over responsibility for the battery, moved the men to Vancouver, where they entered the Canadian Army as a machine gun section in the 2nd Canadian Mounted Rifles. The battery joined the Mounted Rifles when they went to Great Britain in May 1915.

Joe visited his "boys" during the winter of 1915–16, after the battery had been placed in holding units. He enjoyed the time in England, but business called and he returned to the Yukon. By the summer of 1916, however, nothing — including his business — was going to keep Joe out of the fight "over there."

Joe returned to England, determined to take an active fighting role in the war effort. After intense lobbying, and over the opposition of just about everyone in officialdom, he was finally made an honorary colonel in the Canadian militia. The rank had originally been promised to Joe by Hughes in September 1914 as a reward for his donation. However, Hughes had stalled in awarding it to Joe because the regular army officers were worried that as an honorary colonel, Joe would attempt to claim the right to fight overseas with the battery. They were right to worry.

In England, the Yukon Battery was combined with the Borden Battery to make a larger consolidated force. By June 1916, when it was sent to the Canadian Machine Gun School for final training, the Yukon Battery's total strength had declined to 34 men — many had been taken as replacements for other units. In August 1916, the Yukon Battery was recharged with men, Autocars, and other equipment, and was soon on its way to France to join the 4th Canadian Infantry Division. By December 1916, the 1st Canadian Motor Machine Gun Brigade (1st CMMGB) was formed by combining a number of machine gun batteries — including the Yukon Motor Machine Gun Battery.

Canadian machine gunners served in every major Canadian battle, including Vimy Ridge and Passchendaele. They also played a major role in assisting British and other allied troops at many other battles. On June 8, 1918, the Canadian Motor Machine Gun Brigade was divided into the 1st and 2nd CMMGB. The Yukon Machine Gun Battery became part of 2nd CMMGB. By that time, the static trench tactics of the war were changing. The Allied and German armies both realized that to win the war they would need to gain territory.

Both Machine Gun Brigades brought their mobile fire-power to the battlefield during the final German offensive of 1918. The armoured Autocars provided machine-gun support, but their real value was their mobility and speed. Many units during the offensive had reason to thank the boys in the "motors."

* * *

While the Canadian government recognized the contribution Joe Boyle had made to the war effort, officials remained adamant that the honorary colonel could not fight in France — or anywhere else. Joe, railing against the regular officers who were standing in his way, stayed in England looking for any opportunity to get into the fight.

When America entered the war in 1917, Joe helped found a group called the American Committee of Engineers (ACE). Formed by men with engineering backgrounds, the purpose of the ACE was to assist in the war effort wherever and whenever it could. The ACE believed it would be most effective if it operated with a number of subcommittees, and the executives asked Joe to take on Russia's transportation problems.

Soon, Joe was travelling to Russia with the British Railway Mission. In June 1917, he arrived in St. Petersburg dressed in his best new officer's uniform, his chest laden with badges and medals crafted from his own Yukon gold. Regular officers and the Canadian government be damned — if they would deny him his battle glory, he would mint his own!

Joe set to work solving a number of serious transportation problems for the Russians, and had freight and passenger trains moving again in short order. The threat of a German invasion of Russia was thick in the air, but Joe insisted on staying near the front at Tarnopol to complete a surveying project. With no senior Russian officers around, the situation was chaotic as the Germans tried to seize the Tarnopol rail yards. Joe took control as de facto military commander, allowing the city to be held while Russian troops were rushed to the area to create a new defensive line. For his actions, Joe received the Military Order of Stanislaus from the Russian commander-in-chief.

While Joe was taking an active role in the war, the British ambassador in St. Petersburg was sending frantic messages back to London, trying to understand under whose authority Joe was operating. Was he there officially as a British subject, or as Canadian one? The answer that came back from London was that no one was sure.

When reinforcements arrived at Tarnopol, Joe headed for Romania, where rail lines were so blocked that no supplies were moving. He quickly came up with a system using light boats along Lake Yalpukh to get the supplies to an open railway line and into Romania. Using Joe's system, the starving Romanians received several hundred tons of food and medical supplies a day.

Joe soon befriended a British secret agent, Captain George Hill, and the two of them organized a network of over 500 spies to carry out sabotage missions and provide information on German and Bolshevik activities to the British government.

In October 1917, the Bolsheviks staged a final revolution and the government of Russia was overthrown. Workers, freed from the immediate tyranny of the czar's rule, refused to show up for work. Egged on by supporters of the czar who were trying to create anarchy for the new government, the general strike soon had Russia completely bogged down. Food and other supplies were not reaching those in need, and a famine was threatening the whole country.

Remembering Joe's success at getting the trains running again during the war, the Bolsheviks sought him out and asked for his help. Joe agreed, on the condition that they grant him complete control of the rail yards. Recognizing the seriousness of the situation, the local military commander, Nikolai Muralov, gave Joe what he asked for. Within two days, Joe had the Moscow rail yards up and running. It had taken everything from Joe himself working beside the men in the yards, to threatening them with death if they did not work.

Hearing of Joe's success, and of his spy network, the Romanian consul general and representatives of the National Bank approached him to see if he would retrieve the crown jewels of Romania from the Kremlin in Moscow. The crown jewels had been stored in Russia for safekeeping during the war, but now that the Bolsheviks were in charge, the Romanians were desperate to retrieve their property.

Joe was already gathering food and supplies for the Romanians at the request of the ambassador in the newly renamed Petrograd — a delicate enough task in a country struggling to feed its own people. Adding the rescue of the crown jewels, as well as £4 million in Romanian currency, £25 million in gold reserves, and the nation's archives, would greatly increase the danger of this task. Nevertheless, Joe immediately agreed to the request.

He knew the Russians would not give up the valuables without a fight, but he also knew that Commander Muralov owed him a favour for clearing the mess in the Moscow rail yards. Muralov agreed to help, and Joe and George Hill quietly slipped into the Kremlin vaults using a pass provided by the commander. After removing the treasure easily, they faced the more daunting task of getting it out of the country. Their first step was to ferry the jewels, gold, and archives across the street to the Red Cross building, where they placed them in marked Red Cross containers. Next, with 36 boxes in tow, Joe and Hill headed for the supply train that was waiting. Soon the four sleeping berths in Joe's private railcar were full of the treasures of Romania.

Wanting to get out of Moscow quickly, Joe flagged down the first westbound train and attached his private railcar, as well as the 155 freight cars carrying supplies, to it. Just as the train was pulling out, a Bolshevik who had befriended Joe warned him that it would be stopped 80 kilometres out of Moscow and ambushed.

Joe and Hill had only six men with them to defend the entire train on the 2400-kilometre trip to Romania. Taking the threat seriously, the two men climbed up on top of the moving cars and, pistols in hand, patrolled the length of the train.

At a small station 80 kilometres from Moscow, the train shuddered to a stop. From his perch atop the train, Joe saw a number of men working in the dark to uncouple the car carrying Romania's treasurers. Letting out a roar, he launched himself at the men, knocking one of them unconscious. The others fled in the face of the assault, and Joe turned his attention to the stationmaster. The levelled pistol in Joe's hand convinced the stationmaster that the train should be released immediately.

The rest of the trip was just as eventful. On the second night of the journey, a large fire at a nearby vodka factory threatened the train. Joe and the other men did what they could to put out the fire, and ended up removing its fuel source — the train was now full of treasure *and* vodka.

On the third day, a group of Bolshevik cavalry tried to seize the train. Dressed in his uniform, Joe bluffed his way through by convincing the commander that the train was protected by diplomatic immunity and therefore must be allowed to pass. The cavalry stepped aside and the crown jewels were once again on their way.

At Vapnyarka, in the Ukraine, Joe's mission almost came completely undone. A large group of armed Bolsheviks stopped the train. Joe knew he could not win a fight with the group, so instead invited the men to a party in the train station. Soon the thick Russian tea was flowing, fortified with the vodka that had been rescued from the fire the day before.

Once the Bolsheviks had passed out from their tea, Joe and Hill locked them in the station and cut the telegraph lines to ensure that no one could warn others ahead that they had escaped. They then stole a locomotive, hooked up the train, and headed out of the rail yard, crashing through a makeshift Bolshevik barricade as they gathered speed.

Four days after leaving Moscow, Joe arrived in the Romanian capital of Jassy to a hero's welcome and a private audience with the beautiful Queen Marie.

Romania became Joe's war. He had been a supporter of the Bolshevik Revolution when he thought it would make life better for the average Russian. But witnessing the cruelty of the revolution firsthand, and the decision of the Russian government to sign a peace agreement with Germany, disheartened Joe and turned him against the new government. He felt that in Romania he could do some real good.

However, the British ambassador in Romania had the same concerns about Joe as the ambassador in Petrograd. He was soon sending frantic telegraphs back to London asking who controlled Joe. The ambassador felt it was his duty to maintain a delicate balance in the Romanian capital, and he certainly didn't need a brash colonial upsetting the proverbial apple cart. Once again, the British government did not know under whose authority Joe was operating, but instructed the ambassador to do his best to control him. Of course, London authorities might as well have asked the ambassador to hold back the tides — Joe was not going to let a little thing like the British government get in his way.

With the shifting tides of war, the Bolsheviks agreed to pull out of Romania. However, the situation soon became politically volatile and the Romanians were afraid that Russia would attack now that they were not as preoccupied. Further, Queen Marie was concerned that 70 Romanian citizens who were living in the Crimean region had been taken hostage by the new Russian government. Joe was asked by Queen Marie to try to broker a peace agreement. It took all of Joe's natural persuasive power and some help from Bolshevik friends, but he managed to get a peace treaty between Russia and Romania.

Racing back to Romania with the good news, Joe felt very satisfied with a job well done. But to his amazement,

The Yukon Machine Gun Brigade.

the treaty was not welcomed in Jassy. Pro-German forces had been working to convince the Romanian king to sign a treaty with the Central Powers instead.

Joe was especially concerned about the 70 Romanian VIPs who the Bolsheviks were holding in Odessa as hostages. In a private meeting with Queen Marie, he forcefully, but kindly, made his case for the peace treaty with Russia. After three days of backroom negotiating, the Romanian government finally agreed to Joe's peace treaty. On March 18, 1918, Joe was in Odessa, the peace treaty in hand, signed by the Bolsheviks. It was the first peace treaty of WWI.

As part of the peace process, a prisoner exchange had been agreed to — 400 Bolsheviks would be traded for the 70 Romanian hostages in Odessa. The hostages were to board Joe's private train and be returned to Romania under guard. However, politics again reared its head. Upon hearing that Germans had been allowed to cross Romania to fight at Birsla against the Russians, the local Bolshevik commander, Rakovsky, ordered that the hostages be put on a ship that would be heading to the Crimea. They would not be released.

Joe immediately went to the Bolshevik headquarters, only to learn that the commander had left the region. Then, through shear force of will, Joe forced Rakovsky's lieutenant to order the release of the prisoners. But getting the prisoners away from the guards and off the boat was another matter. The disorder caused by the Russian Revolution meant that lines of command were confused at best, chaotic at worst. At Joe's insistence, the guards agreed to parade the prisoners so that he could see if they were all in good health. As the prisoners stood on the dock, nine of them made a break for freedom — two were shot and seven escaped.

Enraged that the guards would open fire, Joe leapt onto the ship, swinging at the Bolshevik soldiers. When order was restored, he refused to leave the remaining prisoners and as a result became one himself.

The ship travelled for three days before reaching the Ukrainian port of Feodosiya. There, the prisoners were taken to a cholera hospital and held. The British vice-consul visited the men, then informed Joe of a rumour that all of the prisoners were to be summarily executed. Working with the consul, Joe came up with an escape plan.

Amidst the chaos that was a constant in the port city of Feodosiya, Joe cut the telephone line and led the prisoners to a boat, the *Chernomore*, which the vice-consul had procured by bribing the captain with 150,000 roubles. As the Romanians approached the ship, some Bolshevik guards challenged their authority to leave. Joe invited the guards onto the ship to show them his pass and then promptly slammed and padlocked the door on the ship's cabin.

The prisoner exchange still had to take place. The arrangement was that the Russians and Romanians would meet in Sulina, Austria, to transfer the prisoners. But when Joe and his charges arrived with no papers or authorizations, the Austrian naval commander refused him access to the port, threatening to destroy the boat and the men aboard. Joe called his bluff and charged directly at the Austrian navy ships, daring them to fire on the "mission of Mercy."

The Austrian commander relented and Joe was finally allowed access to the port. The exchange then went off without a hitch, and Joe was soon renting a barge to take the Romanians to the train station at Galtz and then home.

Joe received a hero's welcome. Queen Marie kissed him, and King Ferdinand embraced him as he was awarded the Star of Romania and the Grand Cross. Newspaper headlines proclaimed him the "Saviour of Romania." Crowds followed him on the streets, and the freed hostages held a dinner in his honour.

Queen Marie and Joe began to spend more and more time with one another — even taking a holiday together at the royal hunting lodge at Cotofanesti. It was at this time that the feisty Canadian became the queen of Romania's lover. King Ferdinand was known to have any number of affairs, and perhaps this emboldened Queen Marie. Whatever her motivation, Joe was a force of nature and had no time for rules that stated a commoner could not be with a queen.

In late 1918, Joe's constant activity and the stress it brought caught up with him; he suffered a stroke. The doctors predicted he would not last two weeks, but figured that if he did, he would be permanently paralysed on his right side. The Romanian royal family then ordered that Joe be moved to the royal summer palace, and Queen Marie personally supervised his care. As Joe recovered, he and the queen spent their days together riding and talking. In the evenings, he told the royal family stories of his Klondike days and sang Irish songs.

Later that year, Marie confirmed on Joe the royal title of Duke of Jassy in the Kingdom of Romania. At the time, Romania was suffering from the effects of the war, and Marie's people were nearing starvation. Recovered from his stroke, Joe offered to visit an old friend in England, chairman of the Allied Food Council, and ask him for food aid to Romania.

It helped to have a royal protector at the end of the war. Joe, who had always been an outsider, was now an international figure. On the way to England, he attended the peace conference at Versailles, then met with Herbert Hoover at the American Relief Administration offices. Upon reaching England, he met with Canadian Prime Minister Robert Borden, who asked Joe his opinion on the state of affairs in Russia. Joe told the prime minister that he felt Russia "should be taken" by the Allies.

Joe returned to Romania, his mission a complete success. He had arranged for nine shiploads of food to be sent to Queen Marie's people. He had also become the head of a small Canadian mission to supervise the distribution of $25 million in aid, which he had obtained for Romania from Canada.

When back in Romania, rumours about Joe and Marie's relationship grew louder and more fervent. (By that point, Joe's marriage to Elma had completely collapsed.) Eventually, Marie was forced to ask Joe to leave, as the politics of their relationship were becoming untenable. Though shocked and hurt, Joe left without any arguments. Shortly after, he took up residence with Teddy Bredenberg — an old friend from the Klondike — in Hampton Hill, England.

Joe passed away on April 14, 1923, at the age of 56. He was buried in Hampton Hill at the St. James churchyard. Queen Marie, who had been to the graveyard as a girl, visited Joe's final resting place in August 1923 and was very disappointed with the condition of his gravesite. Wanting to bestow his resting place with more dignity, she had a thousand-year-old Romanian cross placed on his grave.

In the spring of 1983, after intense lobbying from Joe's family and others, the Canadian Department of National Defence flew Joe's remains home to Woodstock, Ontario. Along with his body, they took the stone cross that had been placed on his grave some 50 years earlier. Queen Marie's words on his tombstone best summarized Klondike Joe Boyle: "A Man with the heart of a Viking, and the simple faith of a child."

Chapter 5

Sir John Craig Eaton and the Eaton Motor Machine Gun Battery

War history teems with stories of fearless generals and steely eyed statesmen who led their nations to victory or were martyred in defeat. But behind the front lines of every war there is a civilian population, stoking the home fires and sacrificing what they can in support of their warriors abroad. These civilians need leaders too, and during the Great War, there was none so stalwart as John Craig Eaton.

John Eaton was born in 1876 to Margaret Wilson Beattie and Timothy Eaton, the founder of Canada's greatest department store chain. As the fifth and youngest Eaton, John was born into a retail empire that was already well established. From birth, he was immersed in a culture of business that included an ingrained sense of civic responsibility.

Growing up, John spent his time either following his

father around the store or fishing and hunting in the woods around Toronto. He received his formal education at Upper Canada College by day, and continued his training at his father's store after school. Before he was even 20, his father sent him on a round-the-world buying trip for the store. On March 23, 1896, John set off by train and ship, travelling first to Japan and spending his 20th birthday in Kyoto. He then continued through Peking (Beijing), Hong Kong, Singapore, and Colombo in Ceylon (now Sri Lanka), went through the Suez Canal, and finished the journey in London. The trip was a singular success, and John proved to both his father and himself that he was an astute buyer and a shrewd negotiator. The trip also stirred a love for travel and adventure that would stay with John his whole life.

At the age of 24, John formally joined the family business as a director, and following the death of his sickly older brother Edward he ascended to the vice presidency. When John asked his father what his role as a vice president really entailed, Timothy asked him if he could say "yes" and "no." When John replied in the affirmative, his father asked if he could decide which to say at the right time. John again answered yes. His father's reply was that as vice president at Eaton's, "that is all you have to do."

John had grown from a curly haired six-year-old into a handsome man. He stood 5 feet, 9 inches tall, weighed about 160 pounds, and, with the full Eaton's stock available to him, was always dressed very well. Indeed, it didn't take long for the Eaton's vice president with the piecing blue eyes to attract the attention of Miss Florence McCrae of Omemee, Ontario. On May 8, 1901, the happy couple were married.

For six years, John continued to learn the retail trade — and when to say yes and no. His father passed away when John was 31, leaving the company, and its presidency, to his youngest son. John's first act was to increase control over the company by buying all outstanding shares from the directors. And the changes didn't stop there.

John brought a new type of marketing to the T. Eaton Company. Not only did he introduce the popular Eaton's Santa Claus Parade, but he also started to use the store's display windows to great effect. John instructed the window dressers to play to the customers' dreams — and his own.

Robert Perry's successful expedition to the North Pole in 1909 was one of the featured window displays. Like others of his generation, John had always dreamed of going on an expedition to one of the earth's unexplored regions. Indeed, the sense of adventure he had acquired from his earlier travels was always near the surface. Though he was one of Canada's richest and most powerful men, John always retained the heart of a child. Among the personal items he valued most in his life was a postcard from Sir Ernest Shackleton on which the great explore had written: "To John from Shack — wish you were here." In an attempt to be included on a Shackleton Expedition, John had promised Sir Ernest $100,000 to explore the Beaufort Sea if the Canadian government would also contribute. John had been extremely disappointed to hear the expedition was cancelled when the government ultimately declined the opportunity.

Eaton's flourished under John's direction. In addition to the buying offices in London and Paris, he opened offices in Manchester, Belfast, Leicester, Berlin, Zurich, Yokohama, Kobe, and New York. He personally drove the company to expand to Moncton, Winnipeg, and other Canadian cities.

His ever-growing empire allowed John to enjoy a lavish lifestyle. In 1910, while his family was on vacation in Europe, he had a large mansion built just down the street from Sir Henry Pellatt's Casa Loma. He named his new house *Ardwold* — Gaelic for "high green hill." When his family returned from Europe and first saw Ardwold, John's two-year-old son lamented that he wanted to go home — he really did not like "this hotel."

John's young son wasn't far off the mark. Ardwold featured 50 rooms, including 14 bathrooms, an underground swimming pool, a dining room, sun porch, music room, library, billiard room, and lounge. The mansion was even equipped with a small hospital complete with two bedrooms for patients, an operating theatre, a room for sterilizing instruments, and another for scrubbing. But for all that, John's favourite feature in the new home was the Aeolian pipe organ. He attached a player-piano-type device to entertain family and guests.

The success of the Eaton's stores also allowed John to

become one of Toronto's most generous philanthropists. When asked, he contributed over $365,000 to build a new wing at the Toronto General Hospital. John was committed to his church, as well. Making no demands for recognition, he offered money to buy land and to build a new church in Toronto. The congregation named the church Timothy Eaton Memorial Church. With so many family members and senior store officials worshipping there, it was not long before local wags dubbed it "St. Timothy and all Eatons."

With tensions rising in Europe, John knew that the world would soon be at war. Out of a sense of *noblesse oblige* that he had learned at his father's knee, John made major commitments to the war effort — even going so far as to open Ardwold to both fundraisers and convalescing troops.

Back in 1908, John, an avid sailor, had purchased a yacht — the *Florence* — for his family and friends to enjoy. Originally built in 1903 as the *Czarina* for Charles Bryan of New York, it had been designed to double as a coast guard vessel if required. The ship had an all-steel hull, was 50 meters long, rated at 237 tons, and had a top speed of 17 knots. With her crew of 18, the *Florence* held a special place at the Royal Canadian Yacht Club in Toronto.

In 1914, John offered the *Florence* to the minister of militia and defence, Sir Sam Hughes, for war use as an armed patrol boat. After being fitted with a three-pound Hotchkiss gun, the *Florence* cruised the St. Lawrence River performing various duties, including anti-submarine patrol. But for all of her speed and performance, the *Florence* was a luxury yacht and not a warship. By September 21, 1916, she was literally coming apart at the seams, with water leaking everywhere. She was costing the Canadian government so much in repairs that it was decided to sell her. The *Florence* was sold, on John's behalf, to a company in the West Indies that pressed her into anti-submarine duties there. In 1917, she either hit a mine or was sunk by a German submarine — the record is not clear.

Without the *Florence*, John no longer needed his high tech ship-to-shore radio equipment, so he donated the gear to the Canadian war effort.

Yachts were not John's only interest — trains fascinated him, too. In 1916, he had the Pullman Company of Chicago design and build a private railway car, the *Eatonia II*, to replace an earlier car built for his father. The *Eatonia II* was 23 meters long and equipped with 4 staterooms panelled in Cuban mahogany. It also featured an observation area, a dining room for 10, a full kitchen, and servants' quarters. But for all its lavish appointments, the *Eatonia II* was frequently pressed into the service of an expected cause — the war effort.

On one occasion, the railcar was rushed to the scene of a dire emergency. On December 6, 1917, John was in his office at the Eaton's store in downtown Toronto when his telephone rang. Thanks to the T. Eaton Company's state-of-the-art communications system, John Eaton was one of the first Canadians outside of Nova Scotia to hear the horrific news: Halifax harbour had been rocked by the most devastating man-made explosion in history.

Halifax was the centre of Canadian shipping during WWI. Everything from food to troops moved through the busy harbour on their way to Europe. That December 6, the French ship *Mont Blanc* — loaded with 2300 tons of wet and dry picric acid, 200 tons of TNT, 10 tons of gun cotton, and 35 tons of benzol — was moving through the congested Bedford Basin when it collided with the Belgian vessel *Imo*. The accident was a minor one, but the *Mont Blanc* broke into flames. Her crew, aware of their deadly cargo, abandoned ship as it drifted closer to shore. Meanwhile, citizens of Halifax, oblivious to the danger, gathered on shore in huge numbers to watch the spectacle of the burning vessel.

Inevitably, the *Mont Blanc* and her cargo exploded. There was almost nothing in Halifax left undamaged. The initial explosion and the following fires destroyed 1600 homes, damaged 12,000, and left 6000 people instantly homeless. Nearly everyone watching from shore perished. They were just a part of the total casualty list, which ultimately reached 1900.

No sooner had John Eaton hung up the phone than he sprang into action. Still feeling disappointment over the cancellation of the Shackleton expedition, John spotted another opportunity to use his wealth and energy — this time to actually save lives. Immediately he committed to send both financial aid and medical assistance.

John's first phone calls were to the Eaton's "family." He called the in-store pharmacist and told him to prepare medicines for the victims, to have them boxed up, and to take them to the train yard where the *Eatonia II* and another railcar would be waiting. He then called in managers from various Eaton's departments and ordered medical supplies, blankets, and food be sent to the *Eatonia II*. The next call was to the infirmary at Ardwold. The two nurses on duty were told to prepare for a long trip.

When the two railcars pulled out of the Toronto station they were loaded to the point of bursting. John, the Eaton's store pharmacist, and the two nurses spent the trip making plans for their efforts in Halifax.

Immediately upon their arrival, John personally took control. He began by searching out a suitable aid station. After a mostly intact building had been found, John and his band of rescuers immediately started unloading the *Eatonia II* while 17 Eaton's volunteers from the Halifax area did what they could to help. The team spent many long, cold days and nights giving away medicine, clothing, and other items to anyone who showed up.

John led from the front — often having to be forced to bed by his co-workers. He was on duty one morning when, just after 4:00 a.m., a lone man, dishevelled and obviously upset, showed up at the Eaton aid station. In a quiet voice he explained to John that when he had returned to his home the previous day, he'd found it in ruins. Concerned about his family, he had begun to dig, and had just finished recovering the bodies of his wife and four children. As H.S. Thornton, a member of the Eaton team in Halifax, later recalled, "I never saw Sir John cry before. He was almost dead from exhaustion himself, but he spent an hour outfitting that poor, sad man."

John stayed in Halifax tending to the needs of the disaster victims until formal government relief systems could take over. When everyone who accompanied the *Eatonia II* arrived back in Toronto they received silver pins engraved with EWS (Eaton Welfare Service) from John himself.

John's contributions to the war effort were not limited to donations from his personal fortune. The T. Eaton Company was one of Canada's largest defence contractors, using its various factories to produce war material. However, from the beginning, the company refused to make money from the war and returned all profits from military contracts to the Dominion government.

Further, the company instituted a policy that any married Eaton's employee who volunteered to serve during the war received his entire pay, in addition to his army pay, for the duration; any single employee received half his Eaton's salary plus his army pay. A total of 3327 Eaton's employees served during WWI. Each had his photo hung in the Toronto store and each drew his Eaton's pay from the company's offices in London or Paris, where savings accounts for the soldiers paid 10 percent interest. By the end of October 1919, the company had paid $2.2 million in war wages.

Eaton's employees suffered 741 wartime casualties, and 238 were killed in action. Those who were taken as prisoners of war received relief packages from the company's office in Zurich.

At home, Eaton's employees contributed to the war effort as well. In total, the T. Eaton Company raised over $4.7 million for the purchase of war bonds. Over 16,000 Eaton's employees subscribed to the Victory Loan in 1918, committing $2.4 million. Company directors contributed another $350,500, and the company itself a final $2 million.

On November 11, 1918, at 2:55 a.m., the siren on the Eaton's building in downtown Toronto announced the end of the war. It was a testament to Eaton's corporate communications systems that the siren sounded in Toronto at the exact moment the armistice was signed in France.

In 1919, as the company celebrated its 50th anniversary, Eaton's hosted a special dinner for 1300 of its employees. Each of the dinner guests was a veteran of the Great War and received a rectangular gold medal emblazoned with the Eaton's coat of arms and the motto *Vincit Omnia Veritas* ("Truth Conquers All"). On the back of each medal was written: "Presented by Sir John Eaton, as a mark of appreciation of service in the great war, 1914-1918." At the dinner, Toronto's mayor, T.L. Church, was quoted as saying: "I wish we had more Sir Johns in the City of Toronto. Sir John is one of nature's noblemen."

Sir John Craig Eaton

* * *

At the outbreak of World War I, it was clear that the weapons and tactics that had worked in the Boer War 15 years earlier were no longer appropriate. The Canadian government found itself short of just about everything but willing volunteers. Sir Sam Hughes realized that Canada's greatest deficiency was in the area of machine guns, and he put out the call for assistance. Like Klondike Joe Boyle, John answered the call and, after discussions with Hughes, agreed to donate $100,000 to pay for Vickers Maxim Machine Guns, armoured vehicles, and uniforms for the yet-to-be-formed Eaton Motor Machine Gun Battery.

The 15 armoured cars paid for with John's $100,000 were constructed in Toronto, where both experimentation and design for the new vehicles were completed. The armoured car guns, which were also constructed in Toronto, were built on a regular truck chassis. The armoured cars were plated with Harveyized steel made from Nova Scotia iron and rolled in Canadian mills. When finally outfitted with pressed steel wheels and heavy rubber tires, the cars could go where infantry and cavalry would have been destroyed by enemy rifle and artillery fire.

On May 5, 1915, despite the protests of the British War Office, which did not want privately funded units on the battlefield, 250 men of the Eaton Motor Machine Gun Battery sailed for England. Prior to their departure, Mrs. Eaton presented the battery with cap and collar badges designed and produced by the T. Eaton Company.

Once in England, the battery got down to serious training. The winter of 1916 found the men in France, assigned to the 3rd Canadian Division. On their way to the front lines, the Eaton battery received new orders. It was to become D Battery, 1st Canadian Motor Machine Gun Brigade. Later in the war, it was renamed B Battery, 2nd Canadian Motor Machine Gun Brigade.

The men of the Eaton Machine Gun Battery were a breed unto themselves. Hand-picked, they were selected for their previous military experience, their versatility, and their cool-headed ability to stay calm, make observations, and formulate plans on the fly. Government propaganda had promised Canadians that the armoured cars, and the tanks they fought beside, were the secret weapons that would hasten the end of the war. The men of the battery believed that given the chance, their armoured cars could deliver on that promise — and so much more.

But like the horse cavalry before them, the armoured cars needed room to run. Unfortunately, for most of the war the Eaton Battery was posted on the Western Front. There, the lines of complex trenches and interlocking battlefields were the opposite of the conditions that would favour the armoured cars. Artillery shells and mining operations churned the rain-soaked land into quagmires of mud that bogged down even the Autocars of the battery.

The Eaton Battery men, who had been recruited under the promise of elite action and superior technology, found themselves stuck in a static fire support role for most of the war. Men who saw themselves as the new cavalry found themselves living in and beside their parked armoured cars, suffering the cold, wet conditions alongside the infantry.

But in 1918, with the Germans in retreat, the war moved out of the trenches. At last, the Eaton Battery came into its own. Intercepted German messages attested to their effectiveness: "All along the roads of approach our troops have been unable to press forward against numerous armoured cars. The enemy have fought with great tenacity to regain Albers and on the Heights of the town sanguinary battles took place supported by the armoured cars."

On November 11, 1918, the Eaton Battery pushed forward over bad roads to the village of Spiennes, securing the sector for the Allies before the armistice was signed. The Eaton Battery finished its war service with the Army of Occupation in Germany, and by the end of the war, the men of the battery had fought in every major battle of the Canadian Army.

For his support of the war effort at all levels, John's name was included as a Knight Bachelor on the 1915 honours list approved by King George V. The award ceremony was conducted that fall at Rideau Hall in Ottawa by the Duke of Connaught, Canada's governor general.

* * *

Even with war raging across the globe, the T. Eaton Company continued to grow. Sales were $22 million in 1907, $53 million in 1914, and $141 million in 1920 — with $60 million of that coming from mail order. The Eaton's catalogue had become so much a part of day-to-day life that a town southwest of Saskatoon, Saskatchewan, was named Eaton by the Canadian Northern Railway.

In January 1922, while in Montreal for a board meeting of the Canadian Pacific Railway, Sir John came down with influenza. When he returned home, doctors immediately sent him to the hospital suite at Ardwold — his flu had turned into pneumonia. For the next seven weeks, Sir John and the doctors fought his condition. Of course, Sir John received the best of care — back in 1919, he had donated $500,000 to endow a chair in the department of medicine at the University of Toronto.

For a time, Sir John's condition improved, but then a general infection set in. He staged a final rally against his illness, and for a while it appeared as though he might recover. But he didn't. On March 30, 1922, Sir John Craig Eaton died at the age of 46.

Throughout Toronto and the rest of Canada, people mourned. Sir John had been a part of the national psyche. All around the world, Eaton's stores, factories, and buying offices closed out of respect. Toronto's elite streamed into the Timothy Eaton Memorial Church for the funeral service, while tens of thousands of mourners waited outside in the cold, hoping to catch a glimpse of the casket as it was brought from the hearse.

At the conclusion of the service, Sir John made his final journey past flags at half-mast and a closed University of Toronto. As his body was carried to Mount Pleasant Cemetery, 25,000 more citizens came to say goodbye, and he was placed in the family mausoleum.

The *Montreal Star* concluded its obituary for Sir John by saying, "Sir John Eaton worked while he worked and played while he played. He enjoyed business and he rollicked in sport. He recognized his humblest acquaintances and he was ever ready to swap a story or perpetuate a joke. His life was constant action, and for weeks at a time he almost lived in his private car. He had few theories and was not strong on abstract ideas. He was a man of action throughout."

Chapter 6

Hamilton Gault and the Princess Patricia's Canadian Light Infantry

ndrew Hamilton Gault was born in England on August 18, 1882. The only son of Andrew Frederick "A.F." Gault, Esq. of Montreal, and Louisa Harman of London, young "Hamilton," as the boy was called, knew only a life of wealth and privilege.

A.F Gault had purchased his first cotton mill in the 1870s, and he soon owned and operated 17, one of which was the largest in North America. As he built his empire, A.F. and Louisa had tried to build a family as well. The couple had eight children but only one — a daughter — survived past infancy. A.F. desperately wanted a male heir to inherit both the family name and the business. When Louisa became pregnant again in 1881, the couple did all they could to ensure a safe pregnancy — A.F. went so far as to promise the Anglican Bishop of Montreal that if the child his wife was

carrying turned out to be a boy, he would build a theological college in the city. In anticipation of the birth, the couple
returned to England. And when a healthy baby boy was born,
the diocese of Montreal received a new theological college
near McGill.

Returning to Canada, the family settled back into upper
class Montreal. When Hamilton was 13, he was enrolled at
Bishop's College School in Lennoxville, Quebec. Based on
the principles of the great English public schools, Hamilton
received a solid formal education. At Bishop's, sports such
as cricket, rugby, and hockey were compulsory. The school's
cadet corps had been established during the American Civil
War as the Volunteer Rifle Company and was the only cadet
corps to service during the Fenian Raids of 1866. While par-
ticipation in the corps was also mandatory, Hamilton joined
more than willingly.

In 1899, Hamilton, at the age of 18, became an officer
in the 5th Royal Scots, Montreal's most fashionable regiment
— and the oldest highland regiment in Canada.

During the Civil War, America's military strength had
raised the concern of annexation with the Canadian government. In response to this concern, Ottawa ordered that a
Montreal militia regiment be formed. Montreal responded to
the call and the regiment grew to a force of eight companies
providing protection on the border between the U.S. and
Canada. From the very first, Montreal's finest sons served
in the Royal Scots, officially formed on January 31, 1862, as

5th Battalion, Royal Light Infantry.

By 1899, rumours of war in South Africa were swirling throughout Montreal. However, there was little chance the Royal Scots would see action in the Boer War. The unit was made up of some of Montreal's richest men and their sons, and to have them on active service for six months or more would have been devastating to the Canadian economy. Besides the 5th Royal Scots were tasked with border duty and the government wanted to keep them close to home.

However, in 1901, Major W. Hamilton Merritt of the Governor General's Body Guard of Toronto recruited a mounted regiment to be maintained at British expense. The Imperial Yeomanry Regiment (later renamed the 2nd Regiment Canadian Mounted Rifles, or CMR) recruited 901 officers and men who would serve in the Boer War as a temporary corps attached to the British Army. Each regiment in Canada was asked to provide volunteers — the 5th Royal Scots sent 2nd Lieutenant Hamilton Gault.

On February 18, 1901, the *Manhattan* arrived in South Africa with Hamilton Gault onboard. His unit was first billeted at Newcastle in Natal, where it underwent an extensive training regimen before transferring to Klerksdorp by train. The men were concerned — it seemed as though the war had passed them by. The Boer forces had been reduced to less than 25,000 and most of the citizens had been moved to British concentration camps.

March 23 marked the first day the regiment would face

the enemy. Gault's unit, E Squadron, travelled light, as their orders were to ride 70 kilometres west through enemy territory to link up with other units. E Squadron moved at a trot, occasionally galloping to cover the distance. Four squadrons linked up and swept the territory. Though few Boers were seen (four killed or wounded, three captured), the operation was considered a success. In all, the E Squadron had travelled 129 kilometres in 23 hours.

On March 31, Gault would witness a battle so bloody it would stay with him the rest of his life. That day, the 2nd Canadian Mounted Rifles were involved in the Battle of Hart's River, or Boschbult. They were attached to a British column, headed by Colonel Cookson, which was tasked with a reconnaissance of the area around the junction of the Brakspruit and the Hart's River. Gault, who was assigned to act as regimental orderly officer, rode with the Canadian commander, Colonel Evans. As a staffer in the squadron, Gault was needed behind the lines, where he would be subject to a grisly spectacle.

At about 10:00 a.m., the scouts patrolling ahead of the column under the command of Lieutenant Casey Calaghan found signs that 500 enemy soldiers and 2 guns were just a few miles ahead. The column changed direction to join up with the scouts and to come in contact with the enemy. Cookson then ordered Evans to wait with the Canadian Mounted Rifles until the supply wagons could catch up.

The column of 60 riders then galloped forward to

capture the enemy guns. But instead of the 500 enemy soldiers they had expected, the column ran straight into the rearguard of an enemy force of 2500. The tiny British force appeared to be overwhelmed.

The supply column that Evans and Gault were waiting for came into view. However, it was shrouded in a cloud of dust and all that could be seen by the Boers were the cavalry outriders. Concerned that the dust concealed a large cavalry force, the Boers held off on their attack just long enough for the British troops to get to Boschbult Farm — a position that could be defended.

As the supply convoy arrived, the men pulled the wagons into a circle, wired them together, and fortified the trenches. About 550 metres to the rear, 200 mounted infantry were under orders to stay in reserve with two machine guns and a pom-pom (artillery piece). Lieutenant Bruce Carruthers with the 3rd and 4th Troops of E Squadron (Gault's squadron) formed a rearguard near the mounted infantry.

The defences were not finished when the Boers, recognizing the supply column for what it was, opened a heavy concentrated fire closing in on three sides of the small British and Canadian force. For three hours the defenders endured the hail of bullets from the rifles of the Boers, but for some unknown reason, most of the Boer artillery shells were duds. Nonetheless, most of the defenders were hit.

Carruthers, sensing trouble, ordered his men to two positions near a detachment of 75 mounted infantry. Suddenly hundreds of Boers crashed head-on into the mounted infantry, who retreated right through the line Carruthers had established. Rather than panicking, Carruthers and 20 men held, forming a curved, single line of men and horses. With no cover, they continued firing until they ran out of ammunition; 17 of the 21 Canadians were either killed or wounded.

At 5:00 p.m., the Boers retreated, unable to dislodge the defenders. The CMR suffered 13 dead Canadians, 40 wounded, and 7 missing. With the exception of the first engagement at Paardeberg on February 18, 1900, Hart's River was the bloodiest day of the war for Canada. It was a slaughter Gault would not soon forget.

The regiment ultimately participated in a number of operations before the war ended on May 31, 1902. Returning to Canada at the end of June, the regiment had proven itself under fire.

* * *

On July 22, 1902, Gault arrived in Halifax just short of his 20th birthday. Colonel Evans, his commanding officer, thought that the young lieutenant had done well enough in battle to be recommended for a position as a regular officer in the British Army. When Gault reached Montreal he received a telegram to immediately join his father in London, where A.F. was hard at work lobbying the war office for Gault's full commission.

Recognizing that his son would not be returning to the family business, A.F. first approached Lord Strathcona and then other high-ranking Canadians. The ultimate answer from the war office was, "Owing to the end of the war there are a large number of officers who have been employed away from their regiments to be absorbed. No more direct commissions to the cavalry can be considered." Gault returned to Montreal and rejoined the 5th Royal Scots.

Some men joined militia units for the camaraderie, whiskey, and cigars, but the 5th was comprised of real soldiers, and on two occasions the regiment was called out to restore civil order. Gault was part of the action on the second occasion. When the ice on the St. Lawrence River opened up in April 1903 and ships could once again ply their trade, civil authorities asked the militia to help deal with riots that were breaking out on the Montreal docks. The troops, responding to a crowd that was throwing rocks and bottles, drove the protesters away.

On July 6, 1903, Gault's father died. A.F Gault's will provided for his wife Louisa, but the large balance of his estate was split between Gault and his sister Lillian, and held in trust. A.F.'s share of Gault Brothers also fell to his son. And though Gault's heart was with the military, he reluctantly took a position at the firm.

Gault was now wealthy — at least on paper. He had a senior position in one of Montreal's leading firms and was a decorated officer of the 5th Royal Scots. No matter how one looked at it, he was one of Montreal's most eligible bachelors. In late 1903, he started to show an interest in a young friend of his mother's. Marguerite Stephens was an attractive and vivacious woman and, despite his feigned indifference, she stole Gault's heart. Within seven months they were married.

Through his 20s, Gault rose to unusual prominence in business and society in Montreal. He even accepted a posting from the Swedish government as consul general for all British North America, with the exception of British Columbia. For two years, his duties ranged from promoting Sweden's trade with Canada, to caring for the interests of Swedish immigrants in Canada. In 1911, with close to 70,000 Swedes in the Dominion, he resigned from his post, arguing he could not give enough time and that a full-time consul general was needed.

As Gault neared his 30th birthday (and control of his inheritance), he realized there was something missing in his life. For him, true fulfillment could only come through heroic achievement — he wanted to embark on an exploring expedition.

Antarctica in 1910 was a siren song for any would-be explorer. In London, Captain Robert Scott was forming a syndicate to explore the South Pole. On February 21, Gault sent a telegram to Scott in London: "Very desirous to join southern party of Antarctic expedition. If application likely acceptable would leave immediately to see you." In response, Scott asked that Gault send his resume by mail.

Despite Gault's extensive backwoods experience, Scott's final reply read: "As you can no doubt imagine it is necessary in selecting members for our expedition to have regard for very special qualifications. I am afraid that your letter does not shew [sic] me that you have the necessary qualification for any of the few important positions which still remain to be filled. With great regret. Believe me. Yours very truly, R. Scott Captain RN." Gault's regret at this response likely gave way to relief and pity when he heard of the failure of the Scott mission and the demise of Scott himself, who froze to death in his tent in Antarctica.

By the time he turned 33, Gault was a captain of the Royal Scots, and, like many of his contemporaries, he was absorbed by the events in Europe. When England declared war against Germany in 1914, he saw a chance to "defeat the King's enemies." Gault knew from his experience in the Boer War that irregular cavalry could perform very well against the enemy, and that they were doubly effective operating against the old-world tactics of the Continental cavalry. However, after discussions with the Canadian minister of militia and defence (Sam Hughes), it was decided that an infantry unit would better suit the needs of the conflict overseas.

On August 3, 1914, Gault offered to provide $100,000 to finance and equip a battalion for overseas service. On August 6, the Canadian government accepted his offer. Authority to raise and equip an infantry battalion was formally granted to Gault on August 10, and it was agreed that any remaining costs would be paid for by Canadian taxpayers through the Department of Militia and Defence.

Lieutenant Colonel Francis D. Farquhar, DSO, an officer of the Coldstream Guards (and military secretary to His Royal Highness, the governor general of Canada), agreed to command the new battalion. Gault would act as second in command. Farquhar suggested that the regiment bear the name of the governor general's youngest daughter, Her Royal Highness Princess Patricia of Connaught. As a result, the regiment was named the Princess Patricia's Canadian Light Infantry (PPCLI). The term "Light Infantry" was chosen because Gault liked the "irregular feel" it gave the regiment.

It has become part of the romance of the PPCLI that the princess took such an interest in "her" regiment, she personally designed and embroidered a banner for the men to take with them into battle. She also designed the crest for the cap and collar badges, consisting of a single marguerite daisy, in honour of Gault's wife, Marguerite.

As part of the original agreement, the regiment could not recruit men from within the active militia. Within 24 hours, recruiting offices for the PPCLI were opened in Montreal, Toronto, Winnipeg, Calgary, and Edmonton. The response was phenomenal. According to the chronicle of the PPCLI written by Ralph Hodder-Williams, "Prospectors, trappers, guides, cow-punchers, prize fighters, farmers, professional and business men poured into the recruiting offices." The majority of the "Originals" were older men, many of whom had seen combat, whether it was in the South African War or as members of the "Legion of Frontiersmen." Only about 10 percent of the Originals were Canadian — the vast majority were of British extraction.

Mobilization of the regiment began on August 11, 1914, and was completed eight days later — a total of 1098 men had been selected, all personally interviewed by Farquhar. On August 23, the men were paraded before Princess Patricia at Ottawa's Lansdowne Part, where she presented them with the unit's colours. The "Ric-A-Damm-Doo," as the banner later became known, was flown on a flagpole cut from a maple tree growing on Parliament Hill.

The Princess Patricia's Canadian Light Infantry left Ottawa for Montreal on August 28, 1914. In Montreal they boarded the *Megantic* — the same ship that had carried the Queen's Own Regiment and Sir Henry Pellatt to the Imperial Exercises in Aldershot. However, sailing was cut short due to enemy patrols in the Atlantic and the regiment soon landed at Levis, Quebec. For the next month, the men of the PPCLI worked on their training and organization. On September 27, 1914, the regiment, including second-in-command Major Hamilton Gault and his wife Marguerite, finally set sail on the *Royal George*. On October 18, they arrived on Salisbury Plain, England.

When British officers inspected the Patricias in November, they were pleasantly surprised. Rather than a force of raw recruits, they found a trained and professional unit ready to go to France — and the front lines. The Patricias were assigned to the 27th British Division as part of the 80th Brigade. They were ordered to leave for Winchester immediately.

On December 21, 1914, the Patricias arrived in France. While the 1st Canadian Medical Corps had been the first Canadians to land in France, the Patricias were the first Canadian infantry unit to do so.

No one was immune from the trials of war. On February 27, 1915, Gault volunteered to crawl around to the rear of the enemy position to fix the location of some German communication trenches. Accompanied by Shorty Colquhoun, the sniping officer, Gault crawled on his hands and knees out between Trenches 21 and 22. It was dangerous enough to be so close to the enemy, but a clear night flooded by moonlight offered no protection for the two Canadians.

Once behind German lines, the two officers split up, with Gault heading off to the left. After covering 180 metres, he turned back to his own lines to report that the area was clear and that he had found no communications trenches. Colquhoun, however, failed to return and was presumed lost.

At 5:15 a.m., buoyed by Gault's information that enemy resistance would be minimal, Farquhar launched a raid through the area between Trenches 21 and 22. Some soldiers jumped into the trenches, killing Germans where they stood; others lobbed hand grenades into different trenches, pulling down the enemy's defences.

Gault was not about to miss the first action of Canadian

troops on European soil — even though as an officer it was not expected he be in the first wave. As he moved towards the action, German flares began to light the sky so that enemy machine gunners could see well enough to find targets among the Canadians. Making his way back to Trench 21, Gault spotted two wounded men in an enemy trench. After finding some medics nearby, he helped load the men onto stretchers, only to find an officer — Talbot Papineau — buried under them. Gault pulled Papineau up from the mud and helped him out of the trench.

As the two officers dove into Trench 21, Gault looked back just in time to see two stretchers bearers, coming under heavy fire, drop the wounded man they were carrying and run for cover. Gault leapt onto the parapet of the trench and, followed by another man, immediately crawled on his belly towards the wounded man. While a stream of machine-gun fire targeted the two Canadians, Gault grabbed the wounded man, rolled into a ditch, and then dragged him to a hedge where medics came to assist. At that moment, a machine-gun bullet smashed into Gault's wrist, shattering it.

Later, Agar Adamson, who was in charge of Trench 21, would write to his wife:

"Though badly hit in the wrist, [Gault] still carried on for 24 hours until the Commanding Officer insisted upon his going back to England for treatment. As Keenan [the Medical Officer] said, complications were sure to set in if he did not get absolute rest. It

almost took force to get him to go. He has played the game magnificently, crawling from trench to trench to trench and cheering up the men ... Cameron and I have written a report on Gault's action ... which I hope will get him the VC (Victoria Cross) as he certainly deserves it. He thoroughly realized that certain 1000 to 1 chance he was taking of certain death and did it. I thought of doing it myself, but was not man or mad enough to attempt it. So sure did I feel that it was certain death that I almost decided to shoot Gault in the leg to prevent him doing it."

Within days, Gault was in hospital in England recovering from what was described as a "gunshot wound, right arm, severe." He would not receive the Victoria Cross for his actions, but the next best thing: the Distinguished Service Order.

On March 20, 1915, Colonel Farquhar was killed by a stray bullet, and Lieutenant Colonel H.C. Buller took over command of the Princess Patricia's Canadian Light Infantry. However, at the second battle of Ypres on May 5, 1915, Buller lost an eye due to a shell fragment. Command then fell to the next most senior officer. Major Hamilton Gault, who had recovered from his injury and returned to France, was now in command of his regiment.

On May 7, as the Patricias moved into what Gault believed were poorly constructed trenches, the Germans opened fire with a barrage of heavy artillery. Gault's concerns about the trenches were well founded. The Patricias were instantly buried as the trenches collapsed under the German onslaught.

Late into the night Gault moved among the Patricias, encouraging them and helping them dig themselves out and reinforce the shallow trenches. Finally, at 2:00 a.m., he lay among the roots of a tree and fell asleep. At 6:00 a.m. he was rocked from his slumber by the crash of German shells. Recognizing that the shells were the sign of an attack, he prepared his men for the battle to come.

At 7:00 a.m., the Battle of Frezenberg had begun. The ridge on which the Patricias were entrenched exploded as though they were sitting on top of a volcano. The earth itself trembled from the impact of heavy artillery. Trenches, newly rebuilt, collapsed again, and the front line ceased to exist. The communications trench was destroyed, cutting off the communication lines to both brigade headquarters and the reserve units. Then, immediately following the collapse of the communication trench, two out of four machine guns were destroyed, severely limiting the unit's firepower.

Gault, facing a wall of German attackers, threw everyone who could walk or crawl to the ramparts with rifles and pistols in hand. At 9:00 a.m., after a brief, unearthly silence, the German infantry were among the Patricias. As Gault looked to the trenches a German shell exploded at his feet, throwing him into the air and then crashing him to the ground. Gault felt for his left leg and found only a mass of torn and bleeding flesh where his thigh had once been. He tried to rise, collapsed from the pain and, before passing out, passed command to Agar Adamson.

The intensity of the German attack meant that no one could help Gault beyond binding his wounds. A medical orderly who tried to assist later wrote of Gault: "I never saw his equal for true grit ... He lay all day with his body torn and bleeding, and it was only at night when the stretcher bearers could approach the trench to get out the wounded that he was carried away, and then he went last, absolutely refusing to go before the worst of the other cases had been taken. He was cheerful and grinning all over when we got him in our dressing station, and kept on grinning when we pulled the blood soaked and ragged edge of his coat and trousers and underclothing out of his torn and lacerated flesh wounds — into which, by the way, you could stick your fist. It will be months before he will be back again."

With their commanding officer out of the fight, the PPCLI now faced a renewed German infantry attack, which advanced behind clouds of poison gas. The Patricias held the front despite being under fire from three sides. The battle was a terrible mauling. When Lieutenant Hugh Niven (who had been given command when Adamson was wounded) and the Patricias were finally relieved, only 154 men were still able to fight, and 700 were dead, wounded, or missing in action.

On December 22, 1915, reinforced with new recruits

drawn for universities across Canada, the PPCLI became part of the newly formed 3rd Canadian Division as a unit of the 7th Brigade.

By May 1916, Gault was fully recovered and back with the PPCLI again as second in command. His regiment was in Belgium holding an important tactical position at Sanctuary Wood. On June 2, the German Army began a concentrated attack on the PPCLI, an attack that began with an artillery strike on the "University Men."

The artillery fire isolated the PPCLI, cutting them off from all communication with the rear. As the German infantry attacked, desperate hand-to-hand fighting broke out in the communication trenches. The PPCLI fought throughout the day and, like at Frezenberg, the toll was high. No. 3 Company was reduced in strength by half, and No. 2 Company had all of its officers either wounded or killed. The commanding officer Colonel Buller, was killed leading a relief of those defending the communication trenches.

The Germans attacked three times during the night of June 2, and three times the PPCLI held. However, by daybreak it was clear that No. 2 Company could not hold out — they were out of ammunition and there was no hope of relief. Under the cover of the last bits of darkness No. 2 Company withdrew across 450 metres of open country under constant enemy fire.

The Germans captured Sanctuary Wood only to be driven out by the 1st Canadian Division 10 days later. For the Patricias, the cost was high. The battalion had suffered 400 casualties with 19 of 23 officers either killed or wounded. Gault was among these wounded — he lost a leg and would never again serve at the front line.

The regiment fought in many actions throughout the rest of World War I and were part of the Canadian Corps that stormed Vimy Ridge on April 9, 1917. In November 1918, the Patricias were involved in pursuing the Germans, and on November 11, 1918, No. 4 Company entered Mons; it was shortly thereafter that the armistice was declared.

Almost five years after its formation, the PPCLI returned to Ottawa with Gault, who had been named commanding officer after the signing of the armistice. On March 19, 1919, Gault "dispersed his regiment into civvy street." The men of the PPCLI were civilians again.

Gault had proven he was no paper soldier. He had commanded the PPCLI in the field and, subsequently, had become their honorary lieutenant colonel. He had been mentioned in dispatches four times (exceptional acts of bravery were included in the daily reports that were sent back to headquarters) and wounded three times. He had also received the DSO in 1915, and was awarded the third class Order of St. Anne, with crossed swords, and the Order of the Crown of Belgium. On January 20, 1920, Gault gave up his command of the PPCLI for the final time. Indeed, he had fulfilled his destiny.

But the war had not been kind to Gault and Marguerite.

Like so many others, the Gaul's' marriage did not survive WWI. Both were guilty of indiscretions and, by 1918, it was clear the marriage was over. Gault and Marguerite endured a bitter, drawn out, and very public divorce at a time when all divorces needed to be reviewed and approved by the Canadian senate. Both of their reputations were damaged, almost beyond repair.

Feeling he could no longer face Montreal society, Gault placed his Canadian business affairs under the control of competent managers. He left Canada, having decided to spend the rest of his life in England. However, he was not above one last gesture. Wanting to remove the last connection of his wife to the regiment, he insisted that the PPCLI's symbol be changed — it would no longer be the marguerite daisy.

In 1922, Gault married Dorothy Blanche, the daughter of E.G. Shuckburgh, Esq. Like Marguerite, Dorothy was outgoing and loved the sporting life. The couple moved to Somerset and purchased a 162-hectare country estate called Hatch Court.

Gault had always been an advocate of Anglo-Canadian unity and felt that he could do much to enhance the relationship between Canada and Great Britain. At a time when citizens of the Commonwealth could run for election anywhere in the Commonwealth they had a residence, he decided to run as a Conservative candidate for Member of Parliament for Tauten and was victorious in the 1924 general election.

His views on national and international issues were well known, and he was respected by political friends and opponents alike. When Gault retired from active politics in 1934, both he and Dorothy were considered to be among the most forward-thinking Britons of their time.

In his free time, Gault enjoyed horseback riding. He was an avid rider, but after he suffered rough falls on two separate occasions, Dorothy insisted that he find a new, safer pastime, one they could embark on together. They settled on flying.

In May 1929, Gault took his first flying lesson in a Gypsy Moth and one month later conducted his first solo flight. In October of that year, he received his pilot's licence. He flew across England and Europe as he fulfilled his duties as an MP. In the 1930s, at the request of the British prime minister, he flew into German airbases to review the Nazi advances in aviation.

Gault never lost his love of nature. Back in 1913, he had purchased 890 hectares of Mont-Saint-Hillaire property near Montreal. He'd enjoyed camping and exploring on his mountain as development continued in the region through the early part of the 20th century. Gault loved the wild nature of the mountain and remained committed to its preservation. By 1957, he was looking forward to returning to Canada and building his dream home on Lac Hertel. But he died before his dream was completed. He left his Mont-Saint-Hilaire property to McGill University with the proviso that the university continue his efforts to protect the mountain for future generations.

Lieutenant Colonel Andrew Hamilton Gault passed away in Montreal on November 28, 1958. His funeral service was held at the Gault family church, St. George's, after which his body was placed on a traditional gun carriage. Led by a military band, officers of the PPCLI and other mourners followed the colonel on his last trip to the cemetery on Mount Royal.

Out of both respect and friendship, Governor General George Vanier and Minister of National Defence George Pearkes were there as honorary pallbearers. Buglers sounded the Last Post as Gault was cremated. Dorothy claimed his ashes and personally took them back to England. Canada's last great Victorian, soldier, and military giant was buried at Hatch Court.

Bibliography

Booth-Martyn, Lucy. *Aristocratic Toronto: 19th Century Grandeur.* Toronto: Personal Library, 1980.

Chambers, Captain Ernest J. *The Governor-Generals Body Guard.* Toronto: E.L. Ruddy, 1902.

Chambers, Captain Ernest J. *The Canadian Militia.* Montreal: L.M. Fresco, 1907.

Chappell, Mike. *The Canadian Army at War.* London: Osprey Publishing, 1895.

Cowan, John. *Canada's Governors General 1867-1952.* Toronto: York Publishing Company, 1952.

Cunniffe, Richard. *The Story of a Regiment.* Canada: Lord Strathcona's Horse (Royal Canadians) Regimental Society, 1995.

Denison, Frederick. *Historical Record of the Governor General's Body Guard.* Toronto: Hunter, Rose & Co., 1876.

Denison, George T., Colonel. *The Struggle for Imperial Unity Recollections & Experiences.* Toronto: The Macmillan Company, 1909.

Denison, John. *Casa Loma and the Man Who Built It.* Erin, Ont.: The Boston Mills Press, 1982.

Gagan, David. *The Denison Family of Toronto: 1792 – 1925.* Toronto: University of Toronto Press, 1973.

Johnson, Major General Sir Louis C. *History of the United Service Club.* London: Committee of the United Service Club, 1937.

Marteinson, John. *The Governor General's Horse Guards - Second to None.* Toronto: Robin Brass Studio, 2002.

McDonald, Donna. *Lord Strathcona: A Biography of Donald Alexander Smith.* Toronto: Dundurn Press, 1996.

McKee, Fraser. *The Armed Yachts of Canada.* Erin, Ont.: The Boston Mills Press, 1983.

McQueen, Rod. *The Eatons: The Rise and Fall of Canada's Royal Family.* Toronto: Stoddard, 1999.

Bibliography

Military Advisory Board. *Canada in the Great War* Volume One. Toronto: Makers of Canada (Morang), Limited, 1917.

Morton, Desmond. *The Canadian General: Sir William Otter.* Toronto: Hakkert, 1974.

Newman, Peter. *Canada 1892: A Portrait of a Promised Land.* Toronto: Penguin Books, 1992.

Oreskovich, Carlie. *Sir Henry Pellatt: The King of Casa Loma.* Toronto: MacGraw-Hill Ryerson, Limited, 1982.

Ronksley, Major P., ed. *The First 75 Years.* Calgary Alberta: Regimental Headquarters – Princess Patricia's Canadian Light Infantry.

Sauerwein, Stan. *Klondike Joe Boyle.* Canmore, Alberta: Altitude Publishing Canada Ltd., 2003.

Stewart, Robert. *Sam Steele: Lion of the Frontier.* Toronto: Doubleday Canada, 1979.

The Scribe. *Golden Jubilee 1869-1919: A Book to Commemorate the Fiftieth Anniversary of the T Eaton Co. Ltd.* Toronto: The T. Eaton Company Limited, 1919.

Williams, Jeffery. *Princess Patricia's Canadian Light Infantry.* London: Leo Cooper, 1985.

Williams, Jeffery. *First in the Field: Gault of the Patricia's.* St. Catherine's, Ont.: Vanwell Publishing, Ltd., 1995.

Willson, Beckles *Lord Strathcona: The Story of His Life.* Toronto: George N. Morang & Co., Limited, 1902.

Acknowledgments

No history is written without following in the footsteps of others. This book is no different, as it depended on writers who lived at the same time as the subjects, and on writers who had the benefit of looking at these men through the filter of time. The following resources were indispensable during the writing of this book: *Lord Strathcona: The Story of His Life,* by Beckles Willson; *Lord Strathcona: A Biography of Donald Alexander Smith,* by Donna McDonald; *Soldiering in Canada,* by Lieutenant Colonel Denison; *The Denison Family of Toronto: 1792 – 1925,* by David Gagan; *Golden Jubilee 1869-1919: A Book to Commemorate the Fiftieth Anniversary of the T Eaton Co. Ltd.*; *The Eatons: The Rise and Fall of Canada's Royal Family,* by Rod McQueen; *Sir Henry Pellatt: The King of Casa Loma,* by Carlie Oreskovich; *Klondike Joe Boyle,* by Stan Sauerwein; and *First in the Field: Gault of the Patricia's,* by Jeffrey Williams.

About the Author

Norman Leach is a historian, freelance writer, and professional speaker from Calgary, Alberta. A graduate of the University of Manitoba, where he majored in Strategic Studies, he focuses on pre-1919 Canadian history — particularly military history. He was named an honorary peacekeeper by the Canadian Armed Forces for his contributions to the Princess Patricia's Canadian Light Infantry. He has written on military, business, and lifestyle topics as well as having been editor in chief of a Calgary magazine.

Photo Credits

Cover: NA-827-2 Glenbow Archives; Collection of Norman Leach: pages 28, 45, 95; Glenbow Archives: pages 25 (NA-3755-11), 75 (NA-827-2); National Archives of Canada: page 72 (C-022940).

OTHER AMAZING STORIES

These titles are available wherever you buy books. If you have trouble finding the book you want, call the Altitude order desk at **1-800-957-6888**, e-mail your request to: **orderdesk@altitudepublishing.com** or visit our Web site **at www.amazingstories.ca**

New AMAZING STORIES titles are published every month.